Khabzela

# Khabzela

by

Liz McGregor

First published by Jacana Media (Pty) Ltd in 2005
Reprinted with changes in 2007

10 Orange Street
Sunnyside
Auckland Park 2092
South Africa
(+27 11) 628-3200
www.jacana.co.za

ISBN 1-77009-080-0
      978-1-77009-080-4

Cover design by Disturbance
Set in Bembo 12/15pt
Printed by CTP Book Printers, Cape
Job No. 000348

See a complete list of Jacana titles at www.jacana.co.za

# Acknowledgments

This book would not have been possible without the help and goodwill of various people: Dirk Hartford and all at Yfm displayed remarkable openness and generosity. DJ Ashifashabba ransacked the Yfm archives to come up with original material from Khabzela. My fellowship at WISER gave me essential time, space and support. In particular, I am indebted to Debbie Posel, Sarah Nuttall and Grace Khunou for reading the entire manuscript and giving me invaluable feedback. Zheng Hai Yao, Ruma Mandal, Fred de Vries and Jon Hyslop read draft chapters. I am grateful to Anton Harber, Sizwe sama Yende, David Coplan, Jonny Steinberg and Francois Venter for illuminating conversations. Tshepo Moloi conducted the interviews with Themba Ndlovu, Naughty Maseko and Zweli Xaba. Phumlani Thwala helped me find my way around Soweto and track down elusive interviewees. My editor at Jacana, Maggie Davey, supplied much needed encouragement and advice through the long and lonely process of writing. Finally, thanks to Fana's family, colleagues and friends for opening their hearts to me. And to my own family and friends for their limitless support.

# Foreword
## to the 2007 edition

When there are so many we shall have to mourn,
when grief has been made so public, and exposed
to the critique of a whole epoch
the frailty of our conscience and anguish,
of whom shall we speak? For every day they die
among us, those who were doing us some good,
who knew it was never enough but
hoped to improve a little by living.

WH Auden: 'In Memory of Sigmund Freud' (1939)

*Khabzela: The Life and Times of a South African* is one of the most important books written since the advent of this country's democracy. In the age of HIV, private grief has become public as parents bury their children. This is also the story of Khabzela. This grief does not recede politely, because every day we continue to bury friends and family.

No conflict anywhere on the planet claims lives on the scale that HIV/Aids does in our country. HIV infection leads to unnecessary suffering and premature death. But death is not the end of suffering. Loved ones (children, partners and parents), colleagues and, in the case of Khabzela maybe millions of young fans, seek an explanation for this death.

But through our answers, this virus exposes the "frailty of our conscience" when we speak of politics, sex, gender, class and race and the HIV epidemic. Our conscience is made fragile because we seek the single cause that explains our vulnerability to HIV infection. In her biography of Fana Khaba, Liz McGregor avoids seeking the single cause of infection, denial, fear and death. *Khabzela* is a moving and complex account of masculinity, culture, tradition, class, race, sex, religion and politics in the age of HIV and Aids.

*Zackie Achmat*
*December 2006*

Raised in Cape Town's Muslim community, **Zackie Achmat** was one of the leaders of the 1976 anti-apartheid school boycotts and was arrested and detained by security police several times. From 1980, he worked underground for the banned African National Congress. In 1990, he discovered he was HIV positive and began working with voluntary community organisations involved with the growing Aids crisis. In 1998, he co-founded the Treatment Action Campaign, which has led the struggle for universal anti-retroviral treatment for Aids patients. He is currently chairperson of the TAC and is widely acknowledged as South Africa's most eloquent and effective campaigner on behalf of those living with HIV. His work has earned him several international awards as well as honorary degrees from South African universities.

# Preface

Fana Khaba died a horrible death. The HI virus had destroyed his brain, leaving him demented and hallucinatory. He could no longer move his arms or legs. He could neither defecate nor urinate. The colostomy bag attached to his bowel to drain his waste was leaking blood. Pus seeped from the wound left by the operation to remove his intestines. A vast bedsore had eaten away his right buttock. More bedsores festered on his back, hips, ankles and elbows.

It must have been a relief to him when, at 12.10 on January 14, 2004, he finally stopped breathing.

He was thirty-five years old.

Fana Khaba's premature death was all the more tragic because it was preventable. Unlike millions of other people with Aids, he was offered the drugs that might have given him another twenty-odd years of healthy life – possibly until a cure was found. But he refused to take them.

I came upon Fana Khaba by accident. In 2003, I was working as a freelance journalist. *Poz*, an American magazine for people living with HIV, asked for an interview with an HIV-positive black celebrity. In South Africa in 2003, black celebrities living openly with HIV were pretty thin on the ground, so when Yfm DJ Khabzela announced on air one day that he was HIV positive, I pricked up my ears. By further coincidence, the CEO of Yfm turned out to be Dirk Hartford, an acquaintance from my university days, and so I was able to secure an interview with the DJ. I wrote up the story and despatched it to New York. In the normal course, this would have been the end of it. Journalism is a short-term affair. You immerse yourself in a story, write it up and then move on to the next one. But this particular tale got under my skin.

A lot of this had to do with my circumstances. I had recently returned to South Africa after a seventeen-year stint abroad and found myself in a radically different country to the one I had left in 1985. I had avidly followed every twist in the country's fortunes from my base in London but, however closely you read every news report and watch every TV broadcast, you will only get the highlights, the broad brush strokes; a version of the truth determined by the direction the cameraman chooses to point his or her lens. The South Africa I found when I returned to live in it bore little resemblance to the one I'd prepared myself for.

So, 2003 was catch-up time. As a young reporter in the early eighties I had been passionately identified with the liberation struggle, but as a white person I entered black townships rarely and fleetingly, always fearful of arrest. Traditional culture was manipulated by the government for its own ends, so those of us opposed to apartheid wanted no truck with it. Now I was in Soweto virtually every weekend, eagerly soaking up every scrap of culture I came across. After years of Britain's homogeneity, the kaleidoscope of rituals, languages and belief systems to be found within half an hour of my home seemed to me endlessly fascinating.

The more I heard about Fana Khaba, the more it became clear that this man had lived every twist of the drama that had transformed my country during my long absence. A child of Soweto, he had grown up in hardship and poverty, the fourth child of seven, brought up by a single mother. Fana surfed every wave that came crashing in with democracy. When public transport was deregulated and the minibus taxi became the chief mode of travel for black commuters and the first industry owned and controlled by black people, Fana was there. He was a taxi driver for several years and deeply immersed in the macho, marginalised culture of taxi drivers. When the airwaves were deregulated, Fana was there – the most popular DJ on Gauteng's most popular youth radio station, Yfm. When kwaito emerged as the beat to which the post-apartheid black youth moved, Fana championed it. And when Aids began to ravish the same generation, Fana caught it and died from it.

In order to understand the central paradox of his death – why he refused the drugs that might have saved him – I understood that I would need to look at how he had lived. And I discovered a life that eerily echoed the fortunes of his country. The man who died in Johannesburg Hospital on January 14, 2004, could not have been made anywhere else but in South Africa in the tumultuous closing decades of the 20th century.

I had three long encounters with Fana Khaba before his death but the virus was already eating away at his brain and not much of what he told me made much sense. I have put together my picture of his life mostly from interviews with his family, his friends, his colleagues and the many members of the medical and alternative healing community whom he consulted during his last frantic attempts to defeat the virus. So, this is a life told in retrospect; through the eyes of other people, with all the gaps and shadings that that inevitably involves.

# № 1

The first time I met Fana, he asked me to marry him. While I was struggling to come up with an appropriate response, he asked if I had any daughters. Then, without waiting for an answer to either question, he declared: "I drive around Soweto and I look at all these women with their HIV-positive children and I think: they're all mine, mine and God's."

By then I was beginning to feel more like his mother than anything else. Tears were streaming down his cheeks. A look of profound loneliness creased his face. I wanted to put my arms around him and tell him everything would be okay. Except of course, it clearly wouldn't.

"God has struck me down with lightning," he whispered. We were having lunch at a restaurant in the Cresta shopping centre, one of the more soulless of the sprawling malls that constitute communal life in suburban Johannesburg. The meeting place had been his choice, not mine. Or, at least, it was the choice of his current minder, an albino named Marlon, who described himself as a 'motivational speaker'. Marlon had initially designated a coffee shop in the centre of the mall but then changed it to a place nearer the parking lot. Fana, he said, was having difficulty walking. When I arrived at the restaurant, a waiter was helping Fana make his slow and painful way to a table at the far end of the near-empty restaurant.

It was my first glimpse of the man in the flesh and I snuck surreptious glances at him as he approached the table and slowly eased himself into a seat. He was tall-ish and slim, but not gaunt. His face was angular, quite dark in colour, and had a mottled appearance. I had barely stammered out my name and what I was doing there when he fired off his marriage proposal. At first I assumed this was to disconcert me, to reassert the power balance between us because I had seen him so weak and frail. When I came to know him better, I understood that he sexualised most interactions with women. But more of that later.

I explained that I was writing an article for *Poz*. Marlon asked if there was a fee in it for Fana. To help feed his children, said Marlon. Apart, presumably, for a small commission for himself. Fana looked down at his plate. I said *Poz* didn't pay for interviews and Marlon let me go ahead anyway, amusing himself with a magazine while Fana and I continued our conversation. Conversation was not quite the correct word. I watched and struggled to extract a narrative as he see-sawed between despair and a manic bravado, only a tenth of which made any sense. All the while, he was hailing waiters with increasingly bizarre demands. "I'm feeling shaky. I need raw garlic!" Then he asked for olive oil. The waiter who brought it broke out in a delighted grin when he recognized Fana. "How are you, sir?" he asked with feeling, touching his hand. His grin revealed a large gap between his two front teeth. "Close the garage door, man!" quipped Fana. The waiter did not appear offended. He walked away, still smiling. A little later, Fana started muttering about amazing grace. I thought at first he wanted to pray over the plate of food that had just been put in front of him but then he urged Marlon to go to the car to fetch the amazing grace. A reluctant Marlon prised himself from his magazine and returned a few minutes later with a plastic bag full of red and yellow pills. Fana swallowed a couple and began to eat. I examined the packet. They were labelled Amazing Grace with the sub-title 'Super Immune Booster. An extract of natures [sic] pure natural herbs. Recommended dosage: two capsules three times a day'. During the course of the next hour or so, I gathered the following information from Fana: that he had had sex with countless women ("sometimes there would be three waiting outside my room while I was busy with the one"); that, as penance for his womanising, he would abstain from sex for three years (there were still two to go); that he had had a difficult childhood and his father had not exactly been a good role model ("I remember when I was a small child telling the police he was hiding behind the stove when they came to arrest him for beating my mother"); and that, despite all the women, he felt deeply alone. "What I want is a soul mate. A woman to live with me, cook with me, pray with me. And when we are sixty, we will retire and run a centre for people with HIV." Dirk Hartford had told me that he was refusing to take anti-retroviral drugs. "Why?" I asked Fana. He pretended not to hear the question.

I felt exhausted when I finally left him: from the inevitable absorption of his pain and distress, and a deep sense of inadequacy. I felt I had merely scratched the surface of a life so different from my own that I couldn't hope to fill in the gaps.

But I was sufficiently intrigued now to want to follow up the story. Preoccupied with other work, I kept in intermittent touch with Dirk, whose emails were increasingly despairing. Fana was on a roller-coaster to self-destruction and no one seemed able to stop him.

The University of the Witwatersrand (Wits) Institute for Social and Economic Research advertised a writing fellowship and I applied for it, suggesting Fana as my subject for research. I got it, and the fellowship started in February 2004 but I knew that by then that Fana would quite likely be dead. In November, I went to see him again. He was back in his mother's house in Emdeni, Soweto, the house he had been born in and grew up in. I did not know my way around Soweto and Dirk suggested I employ the services of Satch, a taxi driver who did a lot of work for Yfm and was a close friend of Fana's. I was to get to know Satch pretty well but my initial impression was merely of a plump, friendly, middle-aged man with an extremely dilapidated car.

On that first trip to visit Fana, Satch said in a speculative way, as if trying out his theory on me: "A man told me that Aids was manufactured by a man named Apollo. He injected it into black people or into things they eat, like oranges. They wanted to kill black people." I said I didn't think that was true; that the generally accepted understanding of the origin of Aids was that humans had caught it from eating monkeys in central Africa; that it didn't make monkeys ill but it tended to be fatal to humans. He waited politely till I had finished speaking and then continued: "This Apollo: he wanted to make money out of making people well again but then he died. They have a cure in New York but they want lots of black people to die first."

I had assumed that my perception of Aids was a universal one: that HIV is a virus that is passed on mainly through sexual intercourse. Once contracted, the virus will replicate itself and it will progressively consume your immune cells, rendering you vulnerable to a variety of illnesses such as meningitis, candida, pneumonia and a form of skin cancer known as Kaposi's sarcoma. Eventually your immune system will give out altogether and you will die. You can, however, take anti-retroviral drugs (ARVs) which will attack the virus and allow your immune system to recover, but they are very toxic, have unpleasant side effects and have to be taken indefinitely. They greatly improve the quality of your life but cannot rid your body of the virus altogether. In other words, individuals have some control over the disease: they can avoid it by changing their sexual behaviour. If they contract it, they can, to a certain extent, fight it off. This conversation with Satch about 'Apollo' was my first indication that the understanding of Aids could be entirely different.

It was just over three months since I had last seen Fana and in the interim he had acquired another minder through whom I had had to arrange the interview. Tine van der Maas, it transpired, had been sent personally by the Minister of Health, Manto Tshabalala-Msimang, to take over the care of Fana. She met us at the front door: a large, barefoot, earthy woman of forty-nine in loose cotton shirt and cotton pants. The outside door led directly into the small lounge, which was dominated by a single bed down the centre, on which Fana lay, propped up on pillows. His body was covered by a clean white sheet pulled up to his chin, but it was evident that he was much thinner than when I had last seen him. His skin seemed much smoother and darker and it had a sweaty sheen, as if he had a fever. He did not remember me but his manner was gentle and very polite. The head of his bed faced the front door which led out onto a small, pretty rose garden. Beyond that was a narrow street, on the other side of which was Zwelethini Higher Primary School, Fana's alma mater. The sound of children shrieking and laughing carried through

5

into the house. But the atmosphere inside was one of barely suppressed panic.

Satch had hoped to make a brief visit, picking me up again later. But he was prevailed upon to stay, most pressingly by Fana who begged him in a hoarse, faint voice not to leave. "This man has helped me," he said. "I remember once I went to a taxi rank and I shat myself in front of everyone." His face contorted and tears seeped down the thin cheeks. "Satch was there for me. Thank you, Satch. So much." His head sunk back into the pillows and he dozed off, clearly exhausted by this long speech.

Satch and I were invited to sit on a couch pushed up against a wall. On the opposite side of the room sat Fana's mother, Lydia Khaba, and a tall, rather scary-looking woman with a scar across her cheek who was introduced as Fana's older sister, Tsidi. I explained that I was writing an article about Fana and Tsidi demanded: "You are going to make money out of this. What does Fana get out of it?"

Tine shut her up: "Now is not the time, Tsidi."

But I thought Tsidi, with her rough straightforwardness, had a point. Her brother's life was draining away before her eyes. They needed all the help they could get. What did I, this strange white woman, have to contribute? Not the cash she had in mind. The fees paid to freelance journalists barely cover their costs.

I felt desperately uncomfortable: the vulture hovering over a dying animal. It was only later that I discovered that I was merely one of a flock.

A couple of weeks before, a picture of a grinning Tine hand in hand with a dazed-looking Fana had appeared in the *Sunday World* with the caption: 'GODSEND Fana Khaba's new minder, Tine van der Maas, has nursed him back from the brink of death by feeding him her special diet.' Since then, a piece in the South African Medical Journal had pronounced her diet ineffectual against HIV and Tine was still seething with indignation. "I keep on saying: if I am a fraud, expose me." Gesturing toward Fana, she declared: "He doesn't want ARVs. I say to him it's not necessary. I say try without it for a month. Then, if you want them, carry on."

Later, much later, when I had obtained copies of Fana's medical records, I discovered that he was at the time of my visit suffering from the following ailments: peripheral neuropathy of the legs and arms; acute, HIV-related colitis which gave him chronic diarrhoea; kidney failure; massive bedsores; and dementia. His CD4 count was 2, which meant his immune system was barely functioning. But Tine was confident she could get him back on his feet with her diet and a tonic called Africa's Solution. The latter came in liquid form and the label on the bottle was the ANC colours of yellow, green and black with a map of Africa and the information that it contained African potato extract enriched with plant steroids, vitamins, grapefruit seed extract and olive green leaf extract. On the back, under the headline: Living a positive life, it advised the consumption of at least two crushed cloves of garlic daily and one cup of Pronutro (a brand of cereal). It was, according to Tine, the brainchild of an Afrikaner biochemist named Professor Chris Barnard, who lived in Bloemfontein. Tine had just received the results of a battery of blood and urine tests she had conducted on Fana and wanted to consult Prof Barnard about them. She strode off to an adjoining room and talked loudly into her cellphone.

Satch took his leave, promising to fetch me later. Lydia Khaba led me into the kitchen where we sat at the counter and drank tea. The kitchen, like the rest of the house, was spotlessly clean and neat. Tsidi's daughter, a pretty girl in early adolescence, came in and took a bottle of water from the fridge. She poured herself a glassful, carefully rinsing the glass in the sink afterwards. There was a sense of order and discipline here that was all the more impressive given the terrible strain the household was under. It was clear that it emanated from the head of the household, Lydia Khaba. Mrs Khaba wore large, square glasses that gave her a slightly forbidding appearance, but her manner was gracious and gentle. She told me that she had borrowed money from the nuns at Kenridge Hospital where she was working, to extend her traditional Soweto matchbox house when her seven children entered adolescence and needed privacy. She was inordinately proud of the fact that she now had two indoor toilets and a dining room.

Mrs Khaba was effusive in her praise of Tine. "Manto phoned me and told me she would send Tine. Since Tine has been here, it has been a great relief. She is so devoted in her work. I am a nurse so I know how devoted she is. I spoke to Manto and I thanked her. I said God had sent her. He [Fana] is getting there. He must just give it a chance.

"I kept on telling him he must go and get tested. I could see in his face he wasn't well. I said to him that I always listen to him telling people that they must use condoms. I said he must go on air and tell them he was positive. I wanted everyone to know. So he and we must be free. Jesus said the truth will free us." Mrs Khaba explained that she was a Jehovah's Witness of the highest rank, a pioneer. Now 74 and retired, her faith has assumed even greater importance in her life. "Every day of my life, I go house to house. If they want to discuss the bible, I sit down and have bible studies with them. I can't do it now because I'm nursing my son."

We were called back to the sick room. Tine wanted to discuss strategy. She had a strong Dutch accent and her speech was punctuated at unexpected moments by a throaty chuckle. "His haemoglobin is only 4.5. Normal is between 13.8 and 18.8. His hands are still white. If he had two units of blood, you would see a different person. It would take two months to get it right our way."

Mrs Khaba: "Can't we build our own blood, using beetroot?"

Tsidi: "That is Fana's decision. My mother is a Jehovah's Witness, not him."

Looking anguished, Fana pleaded: "Can we change the topic please? I will not take blood."

Mrs Khaba said staunchly: "I've had two major ops without a blood transfusion. I trust Jehovah's way."

Tine: "So we go the beetroot and iron route. And your protein is very high. I have to find out where the infection is because then we can give you the right antibiotic. And the CD4 count is not good."

Mrs Khaba asked: "Could the infection be the bedsores?"

"No," replied Tine: "I think it's in the lungs."

Then Satch arrived to fetch me. He wanted a quick word with Tine about his wife's arthritis, which was causing her great distress. Tine listened to her symptoms and then said decisively: "Tell your wife to take lemon juice, olive oil and Africa's Solution. It will not cure the arthritis but she will be acid-free and pain-free in two weeks."

We said our farewells and the Khabas begged Satch to visit again soon. I was delighted to find myself included in the invitation. On the way back, Satch commented on Tsidi's initial aggression towards me: "When we first met, she tried this aggression with me too. I said: you are female. I am male. The 'fe' is added on. You do not have my mental capacity because you are a woman therefore think very clearly before you start any *kak* with me." Satch, I was forced to conclude, was not a new man.

A week later, I visited again and found Fana sitting outside in the early summer sunshine. He was wearing a red shirt and black beanie with the word 'Bacardi' emblazoned in red across his forehead. The sheet covering him had slipped down to expose the nappy neatly tucked around his waist. His chin was slumped onto his chest and his arms lay limply in his lap. Tsidi, sitting beside him, had orders from Tine to make him lift his head so as to exercise his neck muscles. Fana said: "Scratch my back, Tsidi." And Tsidi slid her hand down the back of his shirt. Over the road at Zwelethini Higher Primary, children were playing in the playground. The sight did not bring back happy memories for Tsidi.

"The teachers used to beat us with sjamboks and canes," she said. "I still have scars on my hands." She left school in Standard eight and was pregnant with her first child by the age of nineteen.

Her mother, she said, used to leave for work at 5.30 in the morning. On Saturday, her mother's day off, her stepfather would send her to town to buy meat, using her mother's rail season ticket. "My older sister did the cooking and washing. We were brought up hard. But we are close; we love each other."

Tsidi was the third oldest, born in 1959 to Mrs Khaba and her first husband, who died when she was very young. Fana's father was Lydia's second husband, Petros Khaba, who died in 1972. Fathers in this family did not last long. Like Fana, Tsidi did not have fond memories of Petros Khaba. "Why must I tell lies!" she exclaimed. "He was useless! Lazy!"

Fana's head had drooped back onto his chest and Tsidi lifted it, saying humorously: "He's getting lazy like his father." She gently scratched his back again. "As a little boy, he'd call me to rescue him when other boys were fighting with him. When he told me he was HIV positive, I thought he was joking. When I heard it on the radio, it was a blow. But he's still my brother. Nothing changed for me. Sometimes he's moody. He wakes up shouting but I don't mind. I wash him in the morning; wash his sores, dress him, give him breakfast."

Tsidi, too, was grateful for Tine's presence. "Before Tine came, we struggled. He was very stubborn: he wouldn't eat the right pills. We didn't know what food to give him. When he had meningitis, he wanted to eat pizza." Every now and again, passersby, seeing him sitting there, popped in and greeted him warmly. He seemed barely conscious of them, or of us. Tine came out and said it was time for Fana to have his lunch. She and Tsidi helped him back to bed, carrying his catheter bag. Tine fed him a pinkish liquid. She said it contained liquidised beetroot, ginger, three carrots, tomatoes, spinach, lemon juice, olive oil, pawpaw, watermelon, banana, yoghurt and pronutro. Fana promptly vomited it up.

Yfm was, as usual, playing in the background and we heard Dreshne Pillay, Fana's co-host on the DK@Y show, saying: "Khabzela loves this song. Most songs remind me of Khabzela."

Fana smiled. "Getting a job at Yfm was the happiest day of my life," he said. And, weeping again, said, "there is so much to be done out there. I want to explain to people what Africa's Solution is about. I want to get up and start facing the world positively. I will educate people that they mustn't make love without using a condom."

Tine declared it was time for his exercises. She and Tsidi stood on either side of his bed. On the big TV screen opposite, Mo Shaik, erstwhile financial adviser to deputy president Jacob Zuma, was giving evidence before the Hefer Commission, silently protesting his innocence on charges of corruption. The sound was turned off and Yfm, as ever, was issuing forth from the sound system.

The sheet was removed to reveal Fana's skinny body, naked except for a nappy with the catheter tube protruding from the side. His mouth was very red, presumably from the blood transfusion. Tine had told me that she had persuaded the family to allow him to receive two units of blood a couple of days before. Feeling my gaze, he winked at me, which touched me, this vestige of flirtatious playfulness from that wasted, exhausted body. He looked up at Tine and said: "Tine, I love you." And then looked at me: "I love you too. I don't want you to feel neglected."

I stayed to watch the physiotherapy – mainly because Satch hadn't yet pitched up to fetch me – but wished I hadn't. It was a painful, humiliating process for Fana. Tine insisted it was necessary and she was quite probably correct, but to the uninitiated it looked like sadism. Tine and Tsidi took a foot each and twisted it backwards and forwards. Then each flexed a skinny leg and rubbed his wasted calves. Tine ordered him to lift his arms: "Up! Up!" she cried. One arm trembled slowly upwards and then flopped back onto the bed.

12

Weak as he was, Fana tried to assert himself. "That's enough," he mumbled.

"No, it's not," said Tine. "You're going to do three more, no matter what you've decided. You're making me angry now!"

Finally she gave up, and she and Tsidi donned rubber gloves to change his nappy. Satch, thankfully, turned up and I could leave. It was the last time I saw Fana alive.

# № 2

In mid-December, there was a bizarre article in *The Star*, announcing that 'Yfm DJ Khabzela was given the Nation Builder's Award in recognition of his contribution to the fight against HIV/Aids and his will to live'. In truth, the award was predicated on his impending death. Sponsored by B3 Funeral Services, the prize was a free funeral. A photograph of Fana showed him hollow-eyed and skeletal, too weak even to hold the ostentatious, gold-framed certificate being presented to him by B3.

The award provoked a furious response from his co-presenter, Dreshne Pillay. "All I have to say is that this is not an 'award'," she wrote on the Yfm website. "An award is something you give for an achievement without you benefiting from it as well! My man is fighting with everything he has and no matter how good the intention, the ulterior motive is bigger… the publicity B3 will receive from Fana's funeral is something they could neva have afforded without him! Frankly, I'm infuriated… imagine Fana sitting there watching people plan his funeral. Khabzela loves life and wants to live. TRUST ME the last thing he wants to talk of is his death… everyone like vultures waiting for your death to capitalise on it. How would you feel?"

Batho Batsho Bukopane was a black-owned undertaking business which targeted the black middle classes. HIV/Aids had turned funerals into big business. Bereaved families bankrupted themselves to provide ever fancier funerals for their departed loved ones. A death from Aids redoubled these efforts, as if the fancier the funeral, the more likely people were to forgive the shameful reason for its happening in the first place. And the fanciest funerals in Soweto were provided by B3. They provide a funeral to die for.

Three months before Fana was so publicly given his award, the HIV-positive Sowetan columnist, Lucky Mazibuko, wrote about a similar offer made to him by B3. "When the idea was initially sold to me, I was cynical and perhaps a little offended. Do these people know something I don't? Do they believe my days are numbered?" Despite his scepticism, Mazibuko accepted B3's offer, reasoning "would it not be equally liberating to know that my family is spared some of the expenses that inadvertently accompany the permanent departure of their loved ones?"

In Fana's case, B3 were right in calculating that his days were numbered: he died a month after their visit. At his funeral at Soweto's Orlando Stadium on January 24, 2004, B3's elegant hearses were on display but Yfm also footed a large proportion of the bill. They forked out R210 914. 21 for sound systems, mobile toilets, a goat, cow and sheep to be sacrificed to the ancestors, and lunch for the thousands of people who came to the funeral.

I asked Satch if he could take me and he eagerly agreed. In a subsequent phone call, he confessed to a slight possibility that he might be late: he was on Yfm duty and was required to ferry people, flowers and food to Orlando Stadium. I understood that if I relied on Satch, I'd get to the funeral after it was all over. So I dragooned a friend with good map-reading skills into accompanying me. Satch, as it turned out, was chief pall bearer.

It was mid-summer and we should have been sweating as we buried Fana. But a chilly wind was blowing and we shivered instead. A big white marquee had been erected in the centre of the pitch for family and VIPs. Lean young marshals in jeans, black caps and white T-shirts bearing Fana's face directed some incredibly glamorous young men and women, the cream of the black celebrity circuit, to their chairs. Kwaito stars Zola, Arthur Mafokate and Mandoza were there. So was former Bafana Bafana coach, Shakes Mashaba, and Kaiser Chief's Doctor Khumalo. On either side of the stage, two large images of Fana in a black polo neck jumper, looking very young and rather startled, gazed down on his body, encased in a glossy coffin flanked by banks of fresh flowers.

Fittingly, the funeral was as much performance as service. Top acts such as Mafikozolo, Swazi Dlamini, Thandiswa Mazwai and Joyous Celebration performed between succinct speeches commemorating the man.

When a person dies young and tragically, just as he is beginning to enjoy the success he has struggled long and hard for, and particularly when the hopes and dreams that person embodies resonate through hundreds of thousands of others, one option is to collapse into despair. The other is to try to salvage something positive out of it. That is the generous way of looking at some of the speeches at Fana's funeral. The other way of looking at it brings to mind Dreshne Pillay's image of vultures.

If any proof were needed of Fana's popularity and his pull with black youth, one had only to listen to the speakers who gathered to eulogise him. Almost all tried to harness him to their particular cause. At one end of the spectrum was Treatment Action Campaign hero, Zackie Achmat. Achmat had been HIV positive for several years but, being deeply political, had refused to take anti-retrovirals until the government agreed to provide them for all South Africans who needed them. Like a hunger striker, he had used his own health as the ultimate weapon of protest. Achmat had been prepared to die in order that other South Africans with Aids were given the means to live.

Fana was offered the ARVs but refused to take them. Nevertheless, Achmat found a way of turning him into a fellow Aids activist. He started his speech with the old anti-apartheid rallying cry: "Viva Khabzela! Long live the spirit of Khabzela, long live!" The young people steadily filling up the stands around the stadium roared back in response. "I buy my life for R329 a month. We need to make the government give ARVs to everyone," he said to wild cheers from the stands.

Gauteng MEC for Health, Gwen Ramokgopa, enlisted Fana for another purpose. A general election was in the offing and so far only a third of 18 to 25 year-olds had registered to vote, despite an intense campaign to ensure all eligible voters were on the roll. After commending Fana for having the courage to go public on his status, she said: "His message was for young people to be positive about themselves and about the country. Young people need to be entrepreneurs – that was Khabzela's message." All fair enough. But then she ended by urging young people to ensure Khabzela's legacy "lives on by going out in great numbers" to register to vote. "Fana would have asked you to vote in the election later this year."

And then came the Jehovah's Witness minister who rambled on for at least half an hour at the end, clearly mesmerised by the sonorous dronings of his own voice. He introduced the only jarring note. After a few deeply off-message statements like: "How can a young man keep his life pure? Abstain from sex until you're married. If you've engaged in illicit sex, get tested," the minister made the startling claim that "about a month ago, Fana said: God forgive my sin. Jesus come into my life." I watched the thousands of young people who continued to pour into the stands throughout the funeral and wondered which of those conflicting messages they would leave with when the wake finally ended later that night. What would they have gathered Fana wanted them to do? Fight for ARVs? Register to vote (preferably ANC)? Have sex with only your spouse? Buy a B3 funeral plan?

The fact that Fana was apolitical, didn't believe in ARVs and had sex with hundreds of women he wasn't married to appeared to be irrelevant to his alleged eulogisers. It was his brand that was important and that could now be shaped into anything anyone wanted. Forever silent now, he couldn't contradict any of the claims made on his behalf. But, in a way, he also established the messiness of the message. He was the hustler – inconsistent, promiscuous, opportunist; but at the same time he was very aware of his connectedness to others and what he owed his family and community.

In a final ironic twist, the one woman with whom the minister might have sanctioned a sexual relationship was forbidden entry to the funeral. On the instructions of the Khabas, his fiancée, Sibongile Radebe, the woman with whom he had shared the past six years of his life, was left standing with her family outside the gates of Orlando Stadium.

# № 3

The following day, a haunting picture of Sibongile Radebe appeared in the *Sunday World* newspaper. A black scarf wrapped around her head accentuated the impression of a sorrowing Madonna. With her rounded cheekbones, full mouth and large, soulful eyes, she was clearly a beautiful young woman. And dignified, even in the humiliating position of being left stranded outside her own fiancé's funeral.

What could she possibly have done to merit such treatment? What sin had she committed against him and his family? A couple of weeks after the funeral, I called and asked if I could interview her. She explained that custom dictated that, as a widow, she couldn't leave her home for three months. So I called up Satch and he delivered me to her father's home in White City Jabavu, Soweto. It was a typical Soweto set-up, with an outside loo and a row of extra bedrooms built in the yard beside the old matchbox. But they were sturdy, well-built brick structures and everything was immaculately tidy. One had here an impression of order and relative prosperity.

A serene, smiling young woman dressed in a white T-shirt and track-suit pants came out. Sibongile and Satch greeted each other enthusiastically and he left, promising to fetch me in an hour. I was stern with him: an hour and no more. Sibongile was clearly in a vulnerable state: I didn't want to out-stay my welcome.

Sibongile took me into a spotlessly clean living room. A young man who was visiting her quickly got up and said his goodbyes. Two toddlers she was looking after for a neighbour were shooed outside and we sat down to talk. As in Fana's house, a large television set dominated one wall and the banalities of daytime soap opera competed with Sibongile's recounting of the real-life tragedy that had befallen her.

Sibongile Radebe was only twenty-four years old when I met her. She had recently been through more than most people have to deal with in a lifetime: the death of the man she loved, the discovery that she too had contracted a fatal disease, and a bitter and a public feud with her fiancé's family. Yet she seldom betrayed any bitterness or sense of victimhood. Dark smudges under her eyes and an occasional fit of weeping were the only evidence of what she was going through.

Sibongile was a Soweto girl through and through. Born in Baragwanath Hospital on August 15, 1979, she was educated at Morris Isaacson High School, conveniently situated over the road from her father's house. It was the most famous school in Soweto, epicentre of the 1976 Soweto student uprisings that were the beginning of the end for the apartheid regime. Sibongile knew of those events only as history but she treasured her memories of her schooldays. "I loved school. I was the most famous girl at school, you know. One of those. I took part. I was in the school choir. I was in the debating team. I was the first female president of the Students' Representative Council. I was a peer counsellor for HIV/Aids."

It was while she was still at school that Fana first noticed her. "My sister was hosting a party. Fana was the MC and also a DJ. After the party, he kept calling and calling. He said to me: 'If you find the time, come and see me. I need to speak to you.' I thought maybe he's one of those guys. After I leave, he's going to see another woman and say the same thing. I was brought up to be very alert as far as men are concerned. And I was still a virgin."

When Fana met Sibongile, he was still driving taxis but soon after he got a gig at Soweto Community Radio. Sibongile wanted to be a singer and had made a cassette recording of her songs. "My sister insisted we go to the SCR to promote the cassette. So we got there and we found him and we just talked." A few Sundays later, Fana invited Sibongile to co-host a show with him. "That was the Sunday everything started. After the show, he said: 'Let's just sit outside.' And he kissed me. We never said anything to each other. We didn't say much until the following day. We started talking about the kiss and what it meant. That's when it started."

But Sibongile was still at school. "I thought he was not ready to be in a serious relationship. We were both not ready. So we saw each other maybe once a month or so. My grandmother was a very strict woman. She didn't want any boyfriend/girlfriend stuff. She wanted me to study.

"So at that time, he lived his life and I lived mine, but in a relationship. I suppose he had other girlfriends and, look, he was working for a radio station. He was starting to get famous around Soweto. But in my heart, I knew. He taught me how to listen to music and to find that thing in a song. We loved Anita Baker, both of us. There was an Anita Baker song called 'Baby'. He loved that song. He adored that song. And it was strange. I would play that song and when it had finished, I would be sitting there thinking about him and he would call me, even if he hadn't called me in a month. He would call and say: 'You know what? I am listening to Anita Baker.' And I would say 'Wow, that's funny because I was listening to Anita Baker too.' So that was the connection we had. It was magic."

As soon as she had finished matric, Fana paid *lobola* for her. This was a public declaration that he wanted to have children with her and intended to marry her. They began living together and he volunteered to pay for her to study computer science at Damelin College. In 2000, by which time Fana had achieved the job of his dreams as DJ at Yfm, the couple made the big move out of the township and into the suburbs. They set up home in a smart townhouse complex in Winchester Hills, in southern Johannesburg.

"People always say when you live together, you start realising the differences. But, with me, it was just the easiest thing to do. I enjoyed living with him. I enjoyed waking up with him. Especially Sundays. I would compile the gospel songs he should play on his show. We would sit on our carpet – you see, our house had a carpet – and we'd listen to CDs and sing together. He couldn't sing but he thought he could sing. That was the favourite part for me. That was nice."

Satch's round face popped cheerily through the open door. "You see. I'm on time," he said proudly. We took our leave of Sibongile, with promises to meet again soon. There was much more she wanted to tell me. I heard Satch say something to her about horses and *mlungu*, which I knew meant white people. In the car, I asked him what he'd said. He laughed, slightly embarrassed. "Horses – when the horses come in; end of the month. That means money. I said I'd try to get her some money so she can have driving lessons." From white people, like me or Dirk, I assumed from the *mlungu* bit.

Satch was an indefatigable hustler. He charged me more than twice what he charged Yfm and was forever trying to ratchet up the rate. He was also an irrepressible flirt, constantly hitting on me, but in such a light-hearted and unthreatening way that I was mostly just amused by it. He phoned me up one day to invite me to dinner. "We can go to Rosebank," he said. "You can have Coke. Anything you want!" The fact that he had a wife and four children – that he knew of – didn't seem to constitute any impediment. I said I had a boyfriend. This didn't deter him either. "You must have some variety," he said. "Like white food one night, African food the next night." All this was accompanied by hearty chuckles.

One day, driving back from Soweto, we found ourselves stuck behind a bakkie packed with young black men huddling against each other for protection from the wind. They stared at us quite unashamedly. Satch said: "Look. They think I have a white girlfriend."

"Is that good?" I asked.

"Yes," he replied, grinning broadly.

# № 4

In February 2003, I took up my fellowship at Wits. It provided an office, a phone, a computer, a research grant and a stipend just large enough to cover the bills. Finally I could give up most of my freelance work and devote myself to the unravelling of Fana's life.

It was in the Wits library that my research began. Fana was a Soweto boy through and through, and his development was intimately bound up with its history. I needed to understand the context in which he grew up.

A little over a century ago, rich gold reefs were discovered beneath the bare veld on which modern Johannesburg is built. Miners from all over the world flooded in, in the hope of getting rich quickly. Shanty and tent towns sprung up to house them. Miners were both black and white and overwhelmingly male. The British, motivated by Cecil John Rhodes, fought the Boer leader, Paul Kruger, for control of the Transvaal – and its gold – and won.

The city of Johannesburg began to take shape around the mines and their voracious need for cheap labour. White settlers were given houses and encouraged to bring their families to live with them. Black miners were offered only short-term contracts of between six and eighteen months and had to leave their wives and children in the rural areas. They were housed in single-sex hostels and had to carry passes. Black domestic workers and gardeners were housed in back rooms on their employers' properties. Johannesburg's other black residents lived in slums in the inner city: squalid, dangerous, unhealthy places, that nevertheless had their charms. The nucleus of Nelson Mandela's rainbow nation could be found in the Johannesburg slums of a century ago: Indians, East European Jews, Irish, Brits, Boers, Chinese and Lebanese lived side by side with Africans and coloureds. *Shebeens*, imported from Ireland via the Cape, provided communal spaces from which a rich urban culture emerged, complete with its own music and dialect. Called *flaaitaal*, it was a mixture of English, Afrikaans and African languages. Marabi, a blend of African, Afrikaans and black American-style music, became the signature tune for the dance parties that rocked the slums from Friday to Sunday evenings.

In 1905, the Johannesburg City Council used an outbreak of bubonic plague as an excuse to burn down the so-called Coolie Location, which became today's Braamfontein, home to Wits University, where I sat reading.

And thus was Soweto born. Of the various races living in the Coolie Location, 1 358 people were African. It was decided to create a separate home for them away from the city and so a new African location was established at Klipspruit, thirteen kilometres from Johannesburg. Klipspruit, at the heart of present-day Soweto, was surrounded on three sides by the municipal sewage farm and the stench was overwhelming. To get to work required a long journey in a cattle truck. Not surprisingly, slum dwellers vigorously resisted removal to Klipspruit.

Soweto only acquired its name in 1963 after the City Council offered a £10 prize for the person coming up with the most appropriate name. Suggestions included Oppenheimerville (derived from Oppenheimer, the family which by then controlled the gold mines) and Darkest Africa.

Soweto was essentially a description of its geographic location in relation to Johannesburg: an abbreviation of South Western Townships. Its existence was predicated on the basis that the city and its resources were for white people only. Virtually every further expansion of Soweto represented a new defeat for black people. Yet, paraxodically, it also represented an increased threat to whites. As Johannesburg got whiter, Soweto got bigger. This large and ever-increasing body of black people within striking distance of the city was the stuff of most whites' nightmares. And, ultimately, these fears proved to be justified. It was Soweto which spawned the revolt which eventually shook the country free of its racist rulers.

In the early fifties, Fana's father, Petros Khaba, lived in one of the few inner-city suburbs in which black people still owned freehold. Sophiatown occupied a special place in apartheid iconography. It was a suburb, rather than a township, with a tram and electricity. But most importantly, it was racially mixed, and black people, like anyone else, had freehold title to their properties. In other words, it was a very normal place; the type of community that would have developed throughout South Africa but for the ruling classes' obsession with racial separation.

Although most inhabitants of Sophiatown were African, there were also coloureds, Indians, Chinese and some whites all living side by side. Although parts of it were squalid and over-crowded, it was a vibrant place which attracted the cream of black politicians and artists and became a style generator for urban black culture. The clothes, language and sounds of Sophiatown's streets, nightclubs and music halls were copied throughout the province. The two cinemas in Sophiatown were cultural centres and attracted huge crowds, so it seems reasonable to assume that Petros Khaba had an exciting life: as a cinema projectionist, he would have been in the centre of things. Possibly his position afforded him the power of patronage: the ability to let those he favoured see films for free.

Visitors to Sophiatown cinemas remarked on the boisterousness of their audiences and their uninhibited response to whatever movie was unfolding on the screen. Audiences cheered the bad guy. Cops and good guys were booed. Gangsters were much admired and their clothing styles, mannerisms and sayings emulated. Sophiatown was an aberration from mainstream apartheid culture and its residents drew inspiration from anti-establishment figures everywhere. The siren call of gangster culture was to echo through urban black settlements until well into the new South Africa.

In 1955, the government razed Sophiatown to the ground. With typical subtlety, they renamed it *Triomf* (the Afrikaans word for triumph) and reinvented it as a working-class white suburb. Sophiatown's African inhabitants were forcibly removed to the racial ghetto of distant Soweto. Not only were Africans separated from other racial groups, they were also divided along ethnic lines, in line with government policy to fragment the black community and diminish the threat of a large, united mass of black people.

Petros Khaba, a Zulu, was given a piece of land in Emdeni, a new section on the far west of Soweto. As in neighbouring Zola, only Zulus were settled there. Residents were told to build shacks on their allocated patch of land, alongside which the government would build a house, which would then be rented to them. No African people were to own land.

Petros Khaba's new home was a desolate place. The houses the government eventually built were identical: a monotonous row of basic four-roomed houses which obliterated any attempts at individuality. There were no ceilings, no running water, no electricity. In winter a heavy pall of smog enveloped the township from the coal fires used for warmth and cooking. There were no roads, no parks, no shops, no community centres – and no cinemas. Petros Khaba's skills were redundant in Soweto. Instead, he made wooden boxes to hold coal which he sold to neighbours. But, mostly, it seemed, he did nothing very much and was frequently ill. It was Lydia who kept the household fed and clothed while Petros took out his anger and frustration on his family. In 1972, when Fana was four years old, he died of TB.

Fortunately for his family, his wife, Lydia, was made of much sterner stuff. A few weeks after Fana's death, I invited her to lunch. Satch fetched her from her home in Emdeni and she and I went to Village Walk in Sandton where we inspected the various restaurants on offer to find one which offered what Mrs Khaba fancied eating, which was a nice piece of fried chicken. We looked at menu after menu: there was coq au vin; chicken tikka and chicken à la king. Eventually we found a restaurant that offered roasted baby chicken and she settled for that. Lunch at a fancy restaurant was clearly a huge treat for her and she enjoyed it to the full, ordering the waiter around in a motherly fashion. In Zulu she politely enquired after his health and then had him dancing about, bringing extra bread, water, tomato sauce for her chips.

With the bird nestling in its basket in front of her and everything she needed within range, she looked at me and demanded: "So what do you want to know?"

"I want to get a sense of your life," I said meekly.

In between neat mouthfuls, she told me that she was born

in Phokeng, a village nine miles from Rustenburg in North West Province. The oldest in a family of six children, she was a Tswana by birth. It was only after she married Petros and moved into the Zulu enclave of Emdeni that Zulu became her everyday language. Like her children, she grew up without a father. "I only had a mother. During those days, there was no money. My mother used to give me eggs in a dish to go and pay my school fees. There was enough to eat. They used to plant peppercorn, mealies, beans and pumpkins to eat and sell. And they used to rear chickens and pigs and some cows."

But Lydia had other ideas. She wanted to be a professional, a nurse. After secondary school, she went to a college in Pretoria to study nursing. But in her second year, she became ill; a nervous disorder she said, without elaborating. She dropped out and was forced into domestic service to earn a living.

Lydia married twice and bore eight children, one of whom died in infancy. Her first husband, a painter, died soon after they married. His death, she thought, was precipitated by the paint fumes he inhaled. Soon afterwards she married Petros Khaba, Fana's father. He too was not a strong man. "My husband was ill. He had TB. I had to educate and feed the kids so I went and worked as a domestic worker. "All the time I was dying for a profession. I wanted to see my name on the list in Pretoria of the nursing profession. That's what I was dying for."

I knew that nursing and teaching were the only professions open to black women of Mrs Khaba's generation. Of the two, nursing held the higher status. Nelson Mandela's first wife, Evelyn Mase, was a nurse. As was his cousin,

Albertina Sisulu. It was the profession to which all ambitious black women aspired.

"My sister worked for a doctor who took me to the Kenridge hospital. The Kenridge was a Catholic hospital. I worked for about one month as a ward cleaner and after that I was promoted. They wanted me to go and look after the nuns in the convent. I didn't know anything about nursing so I went to the Red Cross. I used to work and after work, when other people went home, I used to go to the Red Cross. I did my first aid and my home nursing and then after my home nursing I went on with my studies and took my general nursing." For three years, Lydia Khaba worked full-time, did evening classes and brought up seven children single-handed. After Petros Khaba died, she gave up on men. "Men don't want so many children so I decided to devote myself to my children.

"The children were growing and they used to help with the cooking and the cleaning. When I came home, I used to see to a little bit of something and then go to bed. My life was not easy. I've never had an easy life. While I was nursing the nuns at the Kenridge, we had only a four-roomed house. All the kids were in one room. I realised I had to separate the boys and the girls. There was no bathroom. "One day, I asked for a loan. I spoke to the sister who was in charge of the finance there. I said: 'I've got seven children. If I had money, I would extend the house. I would separate the boys from the girls and I would have a bathroom and a toilet inside. My children must see these things practical in their home so that they wish also in their homes to have these things.' That was the only way I thought I would teach them how to live. And the nuns had a meeting and they gave me a loan."

After she left the Kenridge, Lydia worked at an old-age home. The work pattern entailed seven days constant duty and seven days off. Meanwhile, the wife of the doctor who had helped her get work at the Kenridge had contracted Alzheimer's and Lydia shared her care with her sister. During her seven days off from the old-age home, she looked after the doctor's wife.

And, throughout it all, she was a devoted and active Jehovah's Witness. She was recruited in 1962. "Someone came to me and spoke about the bible principles with me and studied the bible with me for some time. Jesus Christ, when he was here on earth, asked God to bring his Kingdom on earth. Because man-made kingdoms don't really resolve our problems. We get sick, we get old, we die. During his reign, under his Kingdom, nobody will die; nobody will get sick. The system of things will change. No one will be working under someone. Everybody will enjoy life to the full. So these promises, you know, make you feel secure."

So this, I thought, was the vision which had sustained Lydia Khaba through all her losses and hardships. Even now, retired at last from paid employment, it gave her a sense of purpose. "As a Jehovah's Witness, you work," she said with pride. "You've got to speak to people about God's Kingdom. We've got magazines like *Watchtower* and *Awake* and brochures like 'What Does God Require of us?' And you read those and read your bible and then try to do God's will by talking to other people about the promises that God is making."

What struck me, listening to the story of Lydia Khaba's life was how incredibly hard she had worked all her life. And how driven she was. Apartheid's rulers had made life as difficult as possible for black people in cities: they should not get too comfortable, was the general message. To get to town and back where she worked, she had to walk to the train station and find a place on a crowded train to travel the 30 kilometres to Park Station. Yet she had held down not one job, but two, and completed her education in the evenings. When she finally returned home in the evenings, she had to attend to the needs of her children.

Money would have been extremely tight: her wages would barely have covered the necessities. Even when Petros Khaba was alive, they would have been living largely on her wages alone. I commented on this and she said stoically: "Yes, but it was alright, Liz. What my husband didn't do for me, Fana used to do for me. He used to say: 'I'm going to replace my father. I'm going to do what I can for you. And he used to buy groceries for me.'

Later, Sibongile told me of the crushing burden that the relentless demands of his family placed on Fana. "She was very strong, in terms of raising her children on her own. But the only problem I had with that was the foundation she gave them: it's almost like she brought them up so that they need to pay her back. With Fana she was worse. Maybe because he had lots of money, more money than the others. He would have to pay, pay pay, for this, for that."

But Mpho Mhlongo, Fana's friend from Jozi fm, paid tribute to her as a warm mother. "She had so much love for her kids. She always tried to prove that. She brought them up as Jehovah's Witnesses, under very strict conditions, which is very good for a family, you know, because it gives a family a very strong backbone. And, also she had to go to work at the same time. Fana's mother worked as a nurse, seven days in, seven days out. Some seven days she's not at home, seven days she's at home. So when the cat's not around, the mice play around, you know. You play truant and then you learn the tricks of the township."

What was it like, I asked Mrs Khaba, to bring children up in the township during the turbulent seventies and eighties? She said she remembered 1976 in particular as a terrible period. "People were dying like flies. They used to shoot. Lots of children died like that. You were not safe, even in your own yard. I went to Durban for a holiday. Fana gave me a holiday." Given that Fana would only have been eight at the time, this seems unlikely, but possibly the mythical status Fana had acquired in her mind as provider and saviour had muddled her.

Fana was never political, she said. "He was just neutral. He would never take a stand. But, from a young child, he always wanted to do something with radio. When he was with young children, he used to take them and say: 'I'm the DJ now.' He'd take a stick or something and speak like into a microphone, you know. I think he got that from his father. He always wanted to be a public figure, you know."

By now, Mrs Khaba had picked the fragile bones of her bird clean. As I paid the bill, she summoned the waiter to pack up the half-eaten remains on my plate for her to take home, for her little dog, she said.

Driving home, I mused on my own experience of the 1976 uprisings: 1 400 kilometres and a world away from Soweto, I was an undergraduate student at the University of Cape Town when the students' revolt erupted in the townships of Cape Town. We ineffectually tried to show our solidarity with fellow black students with a march to the township schools from our pristine campus in the shadow of the Rhodes Memorial – tribute to Cecil John Rhodes, that iconic British imperialist. We had barely reached Klipfontein Road when we were surrounded by soldiers and herded at gunpoint into armoured vehicles. We were taken to Mowbray police station and photographed and finger-printed.

The female students – about thirty of us – were then carted off to Roland Street Prison in central Cape Town where we were locked up for the night in a communal cell. Supper was thick slices of brown bread smeared with sticky white margarine; blankets were rough as sandpaper against our pampered skin. Ablution facilities consisted of a solitary toilet in the middle of the room. It was a considerable shock to us, white middle-class princesses all, but our collective spirit was not entirely broken by the ensuing sleepless, miserable night. Early the next morning, two women warders holding back Alsatian dogs straining at leashes – we were flattered that they considered us so dangerous – came into the cell, followed by a tense little man who was introduced as the district surgeon. Did we have any health problems, they asked sullenly. Even though we were on the wrong side, we still had white skins and were therefore to be treated according to the letter of the law. One girl raised her hand: "If I miss out on one day of my pill, I will get pregnant," she said. These were the early days of oral contraceptives and we took them very seriously. The doctor, an Afrikaans man clearly deeply uncomfortable with this brazen evidence of sexual activity, nevertheless dutifully wrote down her brand of pill. Twenty-nine other hands shot up. An hour and a dozen more brands of contraception later – all painstakingly spelt out and recorded – the doctor trailed out, followed by the warders and their dogs. Within hours, we were taken to the Wynberg Court, charged and released.

# № 5

Fana was born in 1968 into a particularly zealous, not to say completely insane, period of apartheid history. The government fantasy that no black person would be a citizen of South Africa, but instead belong to a separate tribal homeland with its own government, was given full reign. The expansion of Soweto came to an abrupt halt as the government decreed that no further money was to be spent on black urban areas but would instead be diverted to the homelands. No more houses were to be built for black people in urban areas. Licences for trading were severely restricted. It now became policy to deny Sowetans permanent rights to live in cities. Leasehold rights were cancelled. Even those with full urban rights could now be expelled if they were unemployed or could not find accommodation. The Bantu Homelands Citizen Act was passed, which compelled all black people to become citizens of the homeland designated for their ethnic group.

So, picture then the life of the young Fana crammed into the four-roomed matchbox house with seven siblings and his parents. His father demoralised, feared and despised. His mother at work all hours of the day and night, trying to keep them all fed, clothed and educated on the wages of a domestic worker, their very existence in the city a precarious, insecure one. The fourth child of seven, Fana would have been just another mouth to feed in a household where his mother's tiny pay packet was barely enough to cover basic necessities. There is little doubt that Lydia Khaba loved her children, but there was precious little time and attention to go round. The young Khaba children essentially had to fend for themselves in a fractured, demoralised community still trying to recover and reconstitute itself in the bleak wasteland in which it found itself.

How did the young Fana deal with it? What were the daily pressures and comforts which shaped his childhood? Kenny Ndaba was Fana's closest childhood friend. I rang him up and suggested a meeting, which he readily agreed to. His choice of meeting place was the Food Court at the Carlton Centre. "A drink at five thirty?" I suggested, thinking that a beer or two might help oil the encounter. Sorry, afternoons and evenings were out, he said. He had to fetch his son from crèche. This sounded so unlike Fana's other friends that I was intrigued. We settled on 11am. Wondering how we would recognise each other, I tried to describe myself — short-ish with short, dark hair — but he didn't seem particularly interested. It was only when I got there that I realised why: I was the only white person in sight.

In the early eighties I worked for the *Rand Daily Mail*, a campaigning daily newspaper which had its offices two blocks away from the Carlton Centre and we reporters regularly lunched and shopped there. The bar of the adjacent five-star Carlton Hotel served as a useful place for meeting contacts. The Carlton Centre was a precursor to the suburban malls which now proliferate throughout South Africa, but at the time it was a novelty. Citadel-like, with its soaring see-through ceiling shot through with muscular iron beams, it had a great central well into which customers ascended and descended via rippling escalators. Downtown Johannesburg was decreed for whites only and the only black people one saw in the Carlton Centre worked there.

Twenty-two years later it was still an elegant, well-maintained shopping mall. But the shops it housed stocked the brands most coveted by the young and trendy: Soviet; Paco Rabanne, MTN and Cell C. Its customers were mostly young, mostly black and mostly glamorous. The Carlton Centre was the place to hang out; to see and be seen. Partly, this was a matter of pragmatism: taxis' first port of call from Soweto was the nearby Metro Mall in the heart of downtown Joburg. Subsequent journeys to the northern, eastern or western suburbs required another taxi and another fare.

Kenny came up to me as soon as I walked in. He turned out to be a small, soft-faced man of thirty with a slightly depressed, anxious demeanour. We bought cool drinks and sat down at one of the tables to talk, surrounded by minimally dressed young girls chattering on cell phones and pretending to ignore the young men eyeing them out.

Kenny explained the reasons for his anxiety: he was basically unemployed and still living in the old family house in Emdeni. Kenny was as steady as Fana was wild. He lived with his wife, to whom he was faithful, and had one child. He would have another only when he had a job which could guarantee him or her a good life.

After matriculating, Kenny worked for various banks in customer-care departments. When the cell phone industry exploded, he got a job with a telecommunications firm. At that time he did the odd contract for Johannesburg City Council, he said, but it could be six months between jobs.

But it soon became clear that there was a deeper reason. Kenny was still trying to recover from the loss of his friend and the traumatic experiences of his childhood. Kenny was happy to talk. To tell his story seemed to offer some catharsis.

And the creation of a narrative to make sense of a seemingly senseless death was a comforting prospect.

Growing up in Soweto, he said, was a terrifying experience. "And we had no counselling to help us deal with it," he said. "In the eighties, we had violence, apartheid and all that. And when we started to relax after apartheid we had Aids. You survived the violence and the apartheid and now you have to fight to survive Aids. But Aids is easier to deal with – just stick to one partner. During the violence, you never knew when you were going to be shot."

Kenny said he initially made friends with the young Fana because he felt sorry for him. Fana was bullied – partly because he, like Kenny, was a Jehovah's Witness, and partly because of his unprepossessing appearance. "He was ugly," said Kenny bluntly. "He had blemishes; a very bad skin. Even at church, the guys would make nasty comments about him. I saw these guys teasing him and thought I must protect him." And even though their lives were to take off in totally different directions once they reached adulthood, it was a friendship which endured until Fana died. The two families were and still are intimately entwined. They belonged to the same Jehovah's Witness church and would have been subjected to the same social pressures.

Sowetans are a religious bunch. Visit the township on any Sunday morning and the entire population seems to be on its way to church. There are grandmothers in floral dresses and straw hats, leading well-scrubbed children by the hand. There are members of the hugely popular ZCC in their flowing green and white robes with silver stars pinned to their chests. And teenage girls in their sexy best heading for the latest trendy evangelical service. This is a religious community and church is as much a social as a spiritual meeting place.

Churches have retained their popularity by being admirably flexible, adjusting to the requirements of their congregations when imported doctrine doesn't work. For instance, most affect some compromise with traditional African spirituality and its emphasis on ancestor worship. And services are usually joyous occasions with prayers and sermons frequently interrupted by exuberant and beautiful singing and dancing.

Not the Jehovah's Witnesses. Their gatherings are austere affairs which rely entirely on texts imported direct and unmitigated from the church's headquarters in the United States. They will have no truck with traditional African culture: ancestor worship and the consulting of traditional healers is strictly forbidden. This rigidity increased the stress levels in the Khaba household at its time of crisis, when Fana was dying.

One Sunday morning I attended a Jehovah's Witness service in Chiawelo, a poor part of Soweto where many people still lived in squatter camps without electricity or running water. But the hall in which they worshipped was a large, modern, well-equipped building. The congregation was mostly made up of middle-aged women and children but the leaders of the service were all men in suits. Worship consisted of readings from the New Testament and the *Watchtower*, followed by an interactive session with the congregation, which basically consisted of a regurgitation of the written texts in front of them. In a two-hour service, there were three brief, subdued hymns.

I was reminded of a chapter in *Long Walk to Freedom*, Nelson Mandela's autobiography. His first wife, Evelyn, became a Jehovah's Witness when the couple was living in Soweto in the fifties. Her conversion, he claimed, was a strong factor in the breakdown of their marriage. He wrote: "The Jehovah's

Witnesses took the bible as the sole rule of faith and believed in a coming Armageddon between good and evil. Evelyn zealously began distributing their publication, the *Watchtower*, and began to work on me as well, urging me to convert my commitment to the struggle to a commitment to God. Although I found some aspects of the *Watchtower*'s system to be interesting and worthwhile, I could not and did not share her devotion. There was an obsessional element to it that put me off. From what I could discern, her faith taught passivity and submissiveness in the face of oppression, something I could not accept."

Even within the spiritually receptive environment of Soweto, the Jehovah's Witnesses were regarded as outsiders, with people crossing the street to avoid their missionaries and their earnest attempts at conversion. As children, Kenny and Fana were required to go to church three times a week, on Tuesdays, Thursdays and Sundays. This – and the house-to-house visits flogging the *Watchtower*, the Jehovah's Witness magazine – made both of them objects of ridicule at school. "There was a lot of teasing: they'd call us 'Watchtower! Watchtower!'" remembered Kenny.

This, however, did not deter him. He was an active and enthusiastic Watchtower. "I was a regular at church so Fana would come along with me. He bought a briefcase for the bible and song book. And when we had a bible study, he would raise his hand to make a comment or answer a question. And he was highly active in building our Kingdom Halls where we meet. Church members would contribute money and whoever had skills of building, paving, bricklaying, plumbing, electricity… we would build it ourselves. And people were working there for free. No outside construction was hired."

It was on a church expedition to Durban that Fana and Kenny bonded. "We spent a lot of time together at the back of the bus. And during the trip, he wanted to control the radio and I also wanted to have control of the radio. We argued, made up and argued again about the radio. And we ended up agreeing that each would use the radio for an hour then the other would use it. This is because we had different types of music that we wanted to listen to. When we came back, we were friends. He started to come and visit me and I also went to his house.

"I can remember him only once wearing short pants – only once in his life. One time he was sleeping over at my house and it was time to go to bed and we had to strip and all I could see were bones. He was so thin we called him 'Skeleton'. He didn't like that very much. He had this thing that he was not good-looking. But if you listened to him talk, you forgot about that. It brought out the beauty in him."

Fana, believed Kenny, developed the humour and quick wit that helped propel him to stardom as a defence mechanism against the relentless teasing he endured as a child. "People would tease him about his big ears and he would tease them back. And we would end up laughing. He wanted to draw the focus away from how he looked." As he grew older, Fana resorted to humour as both defence and attack. The ironic distance he acquired through his increasingly sophisticated use of humour helped him to survive life's hurts and disappointments.

"He never took anything seriously. He would always find something to laugh about. Sometimes I got irritated by this and I would ask him: 'How can you make a joke out of this?' But he taught me never to take anything seriously but to work on it seriously. Let it not distract you from your goal. But try to find something funny in a serious situation.

45

"He had a nickname for almost everyone he knew. Some people knew their nicknames; some didn't because their nicknames were degrading. Even elders in church had nicknames by the way they looked. Even grandmothers had nicknames. People who didn't understand Fana would say he was disrespectful. And many people didn't understand him.

"He was hyperactive. His nickname was 'Hurry up quickly'. When we were building the Kingdom Halls, he was always running around with a wheelbarrow, making jokes and making people laugh. Wherever Fana was, there would be people laughing."

Kenny and Fana both went to Emdeni Junior High School, misleadingly named because in fact it ranged from Standard Six all the way through to Standard Ten, with some 800 pupils. Kenny's first memory of violence at school came in 1981. Since 1976, students had become much more assertive, refusing to submit to disciplinarian regimes. But the principal at Emdeni, a Mr Mkwanazi, had not caught up with this fact and was prone to regularly caning junior and senior pupils alike. "The senior students got tired of this and they held a meeting at which they decided that the caning must stop and Mkwanazi must be chased out of the school. They went to see the principal in his office and the student leader slapped him and then they all started stabbing him. An older woman teacher came in and called everyone to order. She locked the principal in his office and called an ambulance. It took an hour to come but fortunately he didn't die."

Kenny still shuddered at the memory of it. But it was only the beginning. In the eighties, the last, most vicious decade of apartheid, both sides hardened. There was only room for black and white, so to speak. As a schoolboy in Soweto, there was only one side to take – and that was the side of the comrades, the student leaders, most of whom were affiliated to the national black student body, the Congress of South African Students.

"You had to behave as if you were part of the struggle or they would burn your house down," said Kenny. "I personally was involved in things like destruction and stoning of buses. Causing the unrest, breaking barricades. Because at the time I thought it was normal practice. Because if you did not participate you were seen as some sort of informer or maybe as pro-white or that you agreed with apartheid. So one had no choice but to participate. Even though it was not full participation. But just to be visible in those unrests so that some people would say: 'No, Kenny was there as well. So he's part of us.'"

In 1983, the government tried to set up a locally elected council to run Soweto. But it was considered to be a puppet of Pretoria and a massive campaign was organised to boycott the elections. Only 10% of Sowetans turned out to vote. The councillors became targets for the comrades and many were killed. Kenny recalled the pressure to take part.

"If the comrades knew there was an able-bodied young man in the house, they would come in the middle of the night and call your name and rattle your gate. You had to come out and go to attack the councillors' houses. They knew we were coming because we were singing and *toyi-toying*. I was very scared because the councillors had security guards who were shooting live ammunition. It was terrifying. It was also terrible for my mother and sisters because they could hear the gunshots. They would be so relieved when I came home. Sometimes you would lie and say your mother is sick, you can't go. Sometimes they would buy your story but sometimes they wouldn't and you would have to go anyway."

In 1986, a student at Emdeni was killed. Fellow students suspected the killer to be the brother of Kehla Mthembu. Kehla Mthembu was the leader of the Azanian People's Organisation (AZAPO), the black-consciousness-oriented rival to the ANC. Although AZAPO never achieved anything like the popularity of the ANC, the level of political intolerance at the time turned any rival into an enemy. The comrades suspected AZAPO of undermining the ANC on behalf of the state. This may or may not have been revelant in the horrible revenge killing of Kehla Mthembu's younger brother on the premises of Emdeni Junior High School in 1986.

Mthembu junior ran a dry-cleaning business from a caravan in Emdeni. "The students suspected that Mthembu or one of his employees had killed the Emdeni student, so they met and decided to avenge the murder," said Kenny. "Mthembu heard about this and came to the school to plead his innocence. But as soon as he came into the school, the students attacked him with knives. They stabbed him to death. The principal called the police to investigate but most of the students involved had left."

Also in 1986, the consumer boycott of white business was launched. Trade within Soweto at the time was strictly limited: black people were by and large not allowed to open shops or businesses. Therefore Sowetans had to do most of their shopping in the white city. The comrades wanted to hit white business and enforced the boycott in a somewhat heavy-handed way, punishing people seen with goods bought in town. White wholesalers' trucks delivering goods to township shops were attacked. Often they were overturned and the contents confiscated. Taxis were not targeted, said Kenny, because they were black-owned. But government buses and delivery trucks perceived to be white-owned were.

"If someone saw a truck, they would shout 'target' and we would all have to run after it and attack it. The owners put security guards in them and they were seen to be pro-white because they were hired by a white company. They were equipped with birdshot but when their ammunition ran out, they were defenceless. I saw tyres put round the necks of security guards and set alight. I've seen their charred bodies." His sister and brother-in-law returned to Soweto one day with a boot full of groceries from a suburban supermarket. "The comrades took them all out and threw them into the streets. They destroyed everything."

One of the effects of apartheid was to shrink the worlds of those who lived under it. By the eighties, all South Africa's immediate neighbours, except for Namibia, had been liberated: South Africa was in conflict with Zimbabwe in the north, Mozambique to the east and Angola to the northwest. Its borders were sealed off from the rest of Africa. The cultural, sport and economic boycotts isolated it from the developed world. But even within the country, people were confined to ever-diminishing patches of territory. Kenny and Fana could not easily move beyond the borders of Soweto. But, in practice, they could also not move much beyond their own block because of the stranglehold of rival gangs. The gangs controlled the streets. To varying degrees, this dance with the gangs seemed to have absorbed almost every boy growing up in Soweto. Emdeni and neighbouring Zola were particularly gang-infested.

"If you are from one territory, you can't go to another territory," said Kenny. "A territory is a block of houses. For instance, if you come from the fourteens, you can't go to the fifteens. If you do go there, you won't come back. Girls would be raped. It was hard because some of the bigger shops were in another territory but you couldn't go there. And if someone was killed for being in the wrong territory, there would be revenge killings. There was a lot of competition for cars, clothes, women. You could identify the different gangs by the clothes they wore: e.g. the Fourteens wore All-Star takkies."

In the late eighties, the *comtsotsis* emerged: gangsters who hijacked the struggle for their own ends and were frequently in the pay of the security police. One such group lived near Kenny. "There was a group that claimed to be political activists while using that political activism to commit crime.

"Now Fana had a passion for the English language. Every time he'd speak in English and speak very loudly. At the shops, the taxi rank, inside the taxi, he'd speak only English. Now these *ama* comrades had a base in my street and whenever Fana came to visit, they would threaten him: "Why *ukhuluma iEnglish singa bodarkie*? [Why do you speak English when we are all black?"] Some would threaten to assault him to an extent that he stopped visiting me. But when things looked brighter, they became friends and he would tease them on radio about how they used to threaten him. But the gangsters never harmed us physically.

"There were no-go areas like this area here [in Emdeni] which they call *ama* five (The fives). We knew all the gangsters here. And the comrades were at number fourteens. My house is number 1 459 and Fana's is at 1 409 so we were in the comrades' territory. Unfortunately they died one after the other. And their leader is bound to a wheelchair. They died one by one.

"Whenever he needed to see me, he would take a totally different route so that he didn't pass the house the comrades hung out in."

Fana finally abandoned school without a matric in 1989 and was unable to find a job. A common reaction to this predicament was to turn to crime. Not Fana. "Fana did not resort to crime as many people would do – after passing their matric and without a job," said Kenny. He put this down to Fana's religious conviction, and, more importantly, his mother's influence. Fana's relationship with Lydia was very strong. He always wanted to please her and make her proud of him.

"His mother and my mother were friends," said Kenny. "You don't want to bring embarrassment and disgrace to your family with your behaviour. Because once they see that Mrs Khaba's son is doing this and that, it embarrasses his mother. We all grew up like that. We didn't want to bring embarrassment to our families. And to the religion. Our religion is known for its cleanliness. We would drink sometimes but we would make sure we did it in our rooms. We never went to shebeens or did bad things in public. We made sure that everything we did reflected well on our parents. If one of us decided to do something that would reflect badly on our parents, the one would call the other to order – it could be me or him."

The more I heard about Lydia Khaba, the more I thought what a fascinating character she was. Somehow she had managed to create her own universe free of the moral anarchy that reigned outside it, the gangs on the one side and the predatory, dehumanising state on the other. And her home was where she created that universe.

Sowetan houses were initially presented to their owners as basic, four-roomed shells: without ceilings, flooring, electricity or indoor plumbing. As Soweto became more suburban, and a small elite emerged, internal fittings became a potent source of status. Lydia Khaba came from an elite tribe, the Bafokeng, in what is now North West Province, part of the peasant aristocracy. Later they became rich, due to reclaimed title to platinum mines. In Soweto, Mrs Khaba would have aspired to the same elite status: this might well have entailed shunning tribal traditions, embracing Christianity and the English language. She would have set herself up in opposition to the other powerful female figures of the time, the shebeen queens with their associations with drunkenness and moral laxity.

Extensions to Sowetan houses were forbidden by a state ever fearful of increasing numbers of black people settling in the cities. When the right to extend was finally won, that too became a source of status. A tea set and a dining room would have been essential for the proper entertainment of other ladies of the church. I thought of Lydia Khaba's pride in her dining room, her indoor bathroom and the garage attached to her house. All of these came with considerable financial sacrifice but she felt they were imperative to the proper social and moral grounding of her children.

And with Fana at least, it worked. Kenny's revelation that Fana insisted on speaking English at a certain point in his adolescence was interesting. It must have been while he was still under his mother's sway. Later, at Yfm, he stood out for his refusal to speak English and his insistence on using the language of the streets, *iscamtho*, and his unashamed retention of a strong Zulu accent. Like his mother, he always trod an independent path. He resisted the pressure to become politically active. And even though he admired the gangsters and hung out with them, he never became involved in criminal activities. Like his mother, he retained his own moral centre. But it was a fragile one which took enormous energy and drive to sustain.

As I was about to leave Kenny, he asked me diffidently if I could help with his taxi fare home. During the course of my research, I met and interviewed several young men who, like Fana and Kenny, had come of age with the struggle; the first generation to reach adulthood in the new South Africa. All seemed to have come to it in some way wounded and more or less ill-equipped to meet the challenges and opportunities that came rolling in with democracy. I found it sad that Kenny struggled to muster the R8 required for a taxi ride. He was a thoughtful, self-aware, good man. He deserved better.

Themba Ndlovu has taught history and English at Emdeni Junior High School since 1985. He said he was very surprised when Fana became a DJ: "I always thought he was more interested in church than anything else. He was always talking about church and the bible. Most of his questions were from the bible. It was like *emzalwane* [born again] turning into something else. "Even in his history class," said Mr Ndlovu, "Fana would raise religion. It would come from the blue. That's why I would say: 'Come on, man, you are disturbing my class. Why are you asking such questions?' And he would say: 'I was just making an example.'"

Ndlovu too remembered Fana as the clown figure who used humour to disarm. Fana, he said, was neither rowdy nor rude – "and this was an era when kids were very rude in this area. It was very difficult to have discipline." But nevertheless, he was leader of a group of four or five boys who were disruptive because they were constantly making jokes. "They would turn a serious thing into a joke and in the process they would disturb the class. You would feel sorry for the other guys in the group because they were following Fana and the latter seemed to know where he was going. You could see the boy was clever. But most of the teachers were complaining: 'That group of boys is a disturbance.'

"Most of the people given houses here were Zulus trying to oppose the ANC. There were Zulus in Jabulani and Zola. So the government was trying to build a stronghold for Zulus. In 1986, when the riots started, when the ANC made the call 'make this country ungovernable', while the whole of Soweto was burning, it was quiet here. We were surprised during October, when we were about to prepare for the exams, these kids changed. The riots started here. Emdeni became the most feared area."

During the consumer boycott, South African Breweries trucks would make their deliveries to shebeens around Soweto and come through Emdeni on their way home. "As they were driving through, these kids would run after the trucks, shouting 'target' only to find that it was the end of day and the trucks would be carrying four cases of beer. They would then claim their trucks had been burnt in Emdeni.

"Most of these kids were from KwaZulu-Natal so they were trying to catch up with the struggle. Killings were the order of the day. In room one, there were guns all over."

Mr Ndlovu's memory of the Mthembu killing was slightly different to Kenny's. He believed his relationship with the AZAPO leader led directly to his death. "He pleaded with them, 'I'm not Kehla.' But they killed him in front of us. Everyone started to fear these kids. Even teachers who used to come here for interviews would ask 'Is Emdeni still hostile?'"

Throughout all this, Fana remained the church boy, obsessed with God and girls. But Fana's group were fairly peripheral in the school sub-culture, said Mr Ndlovu. "The main guys around the school were boys who were involved in crime and hijacking. Because, by then, hijacking and robbery had replaced the struggle. Some of our students were involved in robberies and were using our school as a cover. They would dress nicely: those were the boys who were noticeable in the school."

Mr Ndlovu himself was the butt of some of Fana's jokes "He used to call me Bismarck and later he started to call me *Mashaya* [the one who hits]. He would say: '*maar meneer wena uyathanda ukus shaya* [But, sir, you like beating us]." This teasing continued well after Fana had left Emdeni and had become a famous Yfm DJ. "You see, I also sell and deliver sheep and goats. The kids know that and they come to me and make orders for their parents. He used to make jokes about me on the radio. One time, he said: 'Hey *nqishe ngashayiswa yiskoroskoro se van ya teacher Ndlovu* '[Hey, I was nearly hit by teacher Ndlovu in his old wreck of a van.]' At assembly I'd hear the kids saying: 'Hey, Mr Ndlovu, did you hear Khabzela saying you nearly bumped his BMW with your wreck of a van?'"

Zweli Xaba was also at school with Fana. "Emdeni was a difficult place to grow up in," he said. "It was the survival of the fittest. Most of the guys who did not survive were people who did not have a vision; they did not know what they wanted out of life. You see, even when we were involved in the struggle, some of us knew there was life after the struggle."

He agreed with Kenny that there was intense pressure on students to take part. Youth who were not active were regarded as ignorant. "Some people would even look on them as sell-outs. Then there were people who were informers.

"There were student leaders who played a major role in the community meetings, which were mostly held in our school. During the state of emergency, police would come and arrest students during school hours. That created a lot of problems. Because you'd be studying and police would be there. So we would prepare ourselves. When the police came to our school, we would want to know why they were arresting those students. So the school would come to a standstill. Most of the student leaders, especially those who belonged to COSAS, were detained. This really affected our education. I was doing matric in 1986 and we were just told to boycott the exams. On the day we were supposed to sit for the exam, the leaders came into the exam room and said: 'Guys, we are not going to write.' It was hard because we had worked day and night to prepare ourselves for the exams. But because of the unity, we all had to agree we were not going to write. We had strong and very powerful leaders. They said they would arrange [for us to write] I think the following year. But that did not happen. I decided to leave school and work."

# № 6

Fana might have left school without matric but he also left with a very clear idea of what he wanted to be: a DJ. It took him five years to achieve his dream, and in between he had to earn money. There was no room in the Khaba household for slackers and, besides, his own driven, hyperactive personality was not conducive to sitting around waiting for something to crop up.

"He always had a passion for music," said Kenny. "But he didn't have the means for getting into the industry. To make a demo tape, you need to hire music equipment and there was no money for that. And you need to go for interviews – and still there was no money.

"Fana had knowledge about every kind of music – disco, blues, jazz," said Kenny. "We would sit around and listen to music, mostly to the radio. Because I started to work first, I bought Fana and myself a portable radio so that when the old people were watching TV in the house, we would sit outside and listen to music. Obviously there would be some discussion about girls. But mostly it was about music and radio and him getting a job."

Fana's elder brother, Buti, was working for a local businessman called Naughty Maseko, who hired out tents. Maseko was also a long-time Emdeni resident who had known Fana since he was small child.

"When I arrived here in 1968, there were shacks," remembered Naughty. "Then gradually the municipality began building houses. We then moved out of the shacks into the houses. Fana's father was building coal boxes and he would sell them. Fana was still a toddler then. He was the sweetest boy. He was well mannered. Their mother used to take them to church. I think that really influenced him. He really looked up to his mother. Most of the youngsters here in Emdeni got into mischief. But not Fana. After Fana left school, he came to work for me. But one could tell that he had a vision about what he wanted to do. He never wanted to end up in the township doing nothing."

Naughty Maseko acquired his name through being one of those youths who dropped out of school and got into mischief. He was shot by a rival gangster from neighbouring Zola and was paralysed from the waist down. For two years, he was confined to a wheelchair. But Naughty Maseko was an enterprising and ambitious man, determined to make a mark, despite his disability. He hit on the idea of renting out tents for community events such as weddings and funerals. By then he had graduated from wheelchair to crutches.

"Because I'm crippled, I could not put up the tent. Nevertheless, I went ahead and bought my first tent. When it arrived, I just wrote a board and placed it outside my house to notify people that I was now in the business of renting tents. People supported me. I just asked a certain guy to come and help me put it up. We managed, even though it was a bit skew."

As his business grew, he bought more tents and acquired a specially adapted car so that he could deliver them. He employed local boys to help him erect the tents. One of them was Fana's elder brother, Buti.

"Buti worked for me for a very long time. His only problem was that he was quarrelsome when he had one too many. He worked for me and then left, and came back again.

He is now collecting boxes in the streets for recycling. He was the one who brought me and Fana together. I used to have a television and a video recorder and they would come to watch movies. Fana liked to operate the machines. He was the one setting the channels. I realised that he was intelligent and that's how we became friends. I never taught him to drive but he would always watch what I was doing. One day he just decided to take the car and drive."

Fana worked for Naughty Maseko until, he thought, about 1991. "I can't recall exactly when. There was a certain man who lived not far from my place who used to have taxis. From here, Fana went to work for him as a taxi driver." It was not the easiest option.

Taxi drivers are usually young rural men desperate for jobs. The job is ill paid, the hours are long and it is fraught with stress and danger. Taxis are frequently involved in accidents because owners have neglected to fix dodgy brakes or replace worn tyres. Taxi drivers are often first in the firing line when war breaks out over routes. And, as if this were not enough, they are treated with blatant contempt by their customers. They are known as *omageza empompini* (they who wash at the tap) because they get up too early in the morning to wash properly. It is a disdainful term, loaded with sneers at what are considered to be rough, uncouth yokels.

But the contempt is mutual. Taxi drivers are rude to everyone, but women in particular are a target for their scorn. Here are some epithets scrawled on the upholstery of Gauteng taxis:

'If women were good, God would have them.'

'A woman with curves is like a road with curves – dangerous.'

'A woman is subtraction of money, an addition of problems and multiplication of enemies.'

'In the good old days, girls used to cook like their mothers. Now they drink like their fathers.'

Recently, a group of taxi drivers took it upon themselves to teach women a lesson on dress codes. At a downtown taxi rank, they encircled a female passenger, stripped off her clothes and pawed and poked at her near-naked body. Her offence was wearing a skirt they deemed too short. It was not an isolated incident.

And yet the crazed pilots of these coffins on wheels are irresistible to women, young girls in particular. Look into the front seat of virtually any taxi and you will see a pretty girl snuggled up against the driver. Presumably this is economic: the driver can offer a free ride in return for sexual favours and he always has a ready supply of small change from his passengers' fares. Possibly also it is their mastery of the roads. Even gleaming BMWs and Mercedes-Benzes yield before the erratic and manic swoop of the mini-bus taxi. To fail to do so might result in a nasty scratch, a gun to the head, or worse.

Fana joined the taxi brotherhood with gusto. But, true to his independent spirit, he did it on his own terms. Fana was polite and friendly to his passengers. He was impeccably groomed and he kept his taxi spotlessly clean.

Fana's taxi, by all accounts, was a club on wheels but one open to people of all ages. It was where he tried out the latest sound, practised his patter and wooed his women.

Fana was still driving taxis when he met Sibongile. "He would clean it every day; make sure it's spotless," she said. "He would wake up very early in the morning and take a bath and be nice, like he was going to an office. When you walked into his taxi, he would greet you so nicely, you were dazed. So people would always want his taxi. It was comfortable and warm. Sometimes he would just pick up people; maybe go to Sandton and collect Pick 'n Pay staff and take them home. He had relationships with different types of people, whether you were young or old. He was very easy with people."

Mpho Mhlongo, his friend and boss at Soweto Community Radio, said the same thing: "He played good music and when he wasn't playing anything, he was talking to people. Whenever he opened his mouth, something funny was likely to come out."

And despite the fact that he refused to subscribe to the taxi drivers' code of treating passengers like dirt, he still managed to win the love and loyalty of his fellow drivers. I interviewed two taxi-driver friends a few months after his death. It was a Sunday morning and they were at their weekly *stokvel*. Pat Magaela and Simphiwe Mngomezulu were tough, macho men in the old mould, yet their grief and bewilderment at his death were palpable.

We climbed into Pat's taxi to talk. Beer cans were strewn across the floor and the seats were torn and cracked. House music blared from a car radio nearby. Pat Magaela said he first met Fana after he got his break at Soweto Community Radio and had stopped driving his own taxi. "He asked to hang out with us because he loved our beautiful taxis. He drove our taxis whenever he visited us. He made the passengers laugh throughout the journey by telling them jokes.

"He was a crazy man but he was liked by everyone. I will never forget Fana. He was friendly to everyone. He loved girls and he was always partying. He was always going to nightclubs. And he was not scared to mix with gangsters. He loved their lifestyle because most of them are not working. They steal cars. Most of them are rich. He enjoyed hanging with them and talking. He would listen to what they had to say."

Pat and Simphiwe said they worked from 6am to 6pm every day except Sunday, which was their *stokvel* day. They were paid R500 a week. Every Sunday, for eleven months of the year, they would come to the *stokvel* and braai, drink and play music – and put away money, which would be paid back to them in December.

"The biggest source of stress in a taxi driver's life, they said, is traffic officers. The second is girlfriends. This latter complaint was made in a humorous tone but they said that they were deadly serious about it. "You find that somebody goes to work or goes to school. She waits for you every day to transport her. Then maybe you are in love with her because she is always there waiting for you. You are trying to avoid her but she will make sure that she waits for you. Before being a girlfriend, she would pay. But when she is all yours, she won't be paying any more."

Fana loved coming to *stokvels*, they said. "He enjoyed being in places where there was music. He would always want to know which new track was in. He would spend the whole day here. He would come with his ladies."

So, after he became a DJ, this was research for Fana. He would discover what was popular at *stokvels* and then play it on air. This was how he kept in touch, even after he was no longer living in Soweto.

He not only broadcast their music on his show, he also punted their cause. He frequently invited taxi drivers to phone into his Positive Youth of Gauteng show on Sunday mornings and plead their cause with the public. Says Mpho Mhlongo: "He spoke about it so much because he wanted to change people's mindsets. He said these people are so important even though we look down on them. That's why he spoke about being a taxi driver – he wasn't ashamed – so that people should start taking taxi drivers seriously."

Fana did not, however, seem to have made much headway. A discussion on taxi drivers on Yfm chatboards in June 2004, some four months after his death, elicited the following comments from Yfm listeners:

"They are rude and they are Zulu. They say they are the victims of the passangers and I say what the fack you ignorant typical Zulu taxi drivers but when I am on their taxis I stomach every sheet they say because they can beat the hell out of me."

"*Eish mara* taxi drivers are shit. Esp those ones that specialise in hit and runs. Those fucked up matha fuckus know if you get to them they wouldn't be able to pay for da damages."

"Problem wit dem taxis emanates from ppls getting deya licences thru *ama* connexions and dem taxi bosses not payin dem enuff so always dey be in a hurry to get more ppl in de taxi to get deya mani 2 further fatten dem bosses."

"Ever notice how taxi drivers can drive so fast and so badly, be rude and still have time to check people out???? I can't count the taxi drivers who have hit on me while on the road."

"There can only be one solution with these taxi drivers. QUARRENTINE. There must be land bought especially for them. Build rehabilitation centres, some driving schools and a couple of kindergartens where they can be taught some manners."

# N⁰ 7

All the time Fana was working as a taxi driver, he was also trying desperately to get a job as a DJ. "He had built a friendship with the DJs at Radio Bop by phone," said Kenny. "He was a regular caller and they were by now on first-name terms. So we put some money together for bus fare and accommodation and he went to Bophuthatswana [now North West Province]. He came back unsuccessful but they gave him posters of DJs. He brought back some for me as well. And then he started making demo tapes. We would make demo tapes of him broadcasting or reading the news, hosting a talk show or interviewing people. He would interview me as if I was Doctor Khumalo [former Kaizer Chiefs star soccer player].

"Once we hired a whole studio system for the weekend for voice training. We knew his mother was not going to be at home so we put it in his house. We stocked food and drinks because we didn't want any disturbances. We stayed there till Monday morning. And then he went to Capital Radio in the Eastern Cape with those demo tapes. He came back unsuccessful again. He never told me what he felt because he was too stressed to talk about it. And demo tape after demo tape, we tried to find what went wrong. Sometimes it was the English language that was wrong."

Fana was also getting as much practical experience as he could. He and Kenny teamed up with a friend called Jabu who had a camera and a sound system. They called themselves Full Force and offered a package for weddings and birthday parties. Jabu took pictures, both still and video, while Fana did the music and DJ-ing. Kenny was logistics man, making sure it all hung together.

After 1994, the airwaves were deregulated and a number of community radio stations sprung up. Kenny Ndaba heard from a colleague at the Standard Bank where he was working that a radio station was opening in Dube, Soweto. Kenny phoned Fana who hot-footed it down to the nascent station with his demo tapes.

Mpho Mhlongo was one of the founding members of Soweto Community Radio, which later became known as Jozi fm, with Mpho Mhlongo as the station manager. One Sunday morning in April, I headed down to the Khaya Centre in Dube, where the station was still based. Jozi fm was a string of sparsely furnished rooms in a functional office block. In one of the rooms Mpho Mhlongo was approving the playlist with the duty DJ. A plump, glossy-skinned man of thirty-three in Sunday casual track-suit, he led me off to a small lounge. Through a glass window was another room, empty except for a large desk. "That was Fana's," he said. "That was where Fana sat." It was only three months since Fana's death and talking about him still moved Mpho to tears. They started off as boss and employee but became firm friends, he said.

It was Mpho Mhlongo who finally gave Fana his break. "We were not yet on air. We were still struggling to get things going when he heard about us and he came and said: 'Hey man, I want to go on radio.'" Fana told Mpho about his long struggle to get on air. "He'd gone to Radio Bop, to Venda, to Transkei. He would go there and find a R100-a-night hotel that looked very shady and just sleep there for the night and in the morning, he would wake up and go to the station. He tried SABC of course as well, but he failed.

"To be honest with you, Fana never spoke English the way they wanted him to. I don't want to say it was because of his education but he just never spoke much English. If you listen to Yfm, everybody's English and with him, there was always that difference. For every station, you had to have this English thing. Radio Metro you had to speak English. Radio Bop you had to speak English. At other stations, he couldn't speak languages like Tshivenda and isiXhosa." But Mhlongo liked him and gave him a chance.

"We went together to do mock broadcasts. Your mock broadcast would be getting a system and a microphone and a few CDs to play to people in shopping malls. I saw raw talent and nobody wanted to tap into it. I think he was, for me, the funniest presenter ever. He was always making jokes and having fun. He had a sense of humour until he died. He just never lost it. And I think because of that, we clicked. We became friends. Although my position wouldn't allow me to just play around all the time.

"There was a time I had to give him a grievance slot, as a punishment. I thought he would never come and do it because he said: 'I'm mad. I won't do it.' And remember, we're a voluntary organisation. If they won't do it, they won't do it. But guess what? He was here in the morning. It was 3am to 6am and he came to do it. I think it was for about a month. And then eventually I took him back. I think he was getting to be big-headed. He was big-headed, you know. He was a star. He was very popular."

It was with Soweto Community Radio that Fana began building up a following. He started off in the prime Drive Time slot from 4pm to 6pm, the period with the highest listenership. Soweto Community Radio was a voluntary organisation. DJs were given the air time but precious little else. For Fana, this was a minor obstacle. "He was one of the first people to get sponsorship for his programme, from a local businessman called Memzi Mchunu," said Mpho. "And he was one of those who got advertisements first. We used his jingles at the station. He was just stealing from other adverts and putting it together. He got a percentage of the advertising revenue he brought in – 20%. That's how he earned."

He also had to bring in his own music and at that too he shone. "Fana didn't have a lot of music then but he worked with the popular DJs, like Ganyane. Ganyane was popular because he did twelve albums for Simunye Group at SABC1. Fana used to go to Ganyane and borrow albums. So that's why he always had the latest albums because he played music from DJs who were playing in clubs."

It was a time of mutual personal experimentation. In 1996, Mpho and Fana together made the first big move, out of their family houses and into the rented outside rooms that proliferated after the restrictions on extending the original Soweto matchbox houses were lifted.

While at Soweto Community Radio, Fana still occasionally drove taxis. "He actually left the taxi industry. But some weekends and some mornings before he came to work, he'd just take one trip to Bara [Baragwanath Hospital]. He still had friends in the industry. Until the day he died, he still had friends in the taxi industry. He always loved it. Until the day he died, Khabzela drove like a taxi driver."

As I was about to leave, a middle-aged woman came in. Mpho introduced me to her as Rose Khaba, Fana's elder half-sister. A couple of days later, I rang him to get a contact number for one of Fana's taxi-driver friends and he said Rose had told him Mrs Khaba was angry with me because of an article I'd had published recently about Fana in the *Sunday Times* and she wanted me to come and see her.

# № 8

My relations with the Khaba family were never straightforward. I met them under the most fraught circumstances imaginable, at the deathbed of their son, brother and breadwinner. I was always deeply conscious of the tenuousness of my own position in relation to them. Their and Fana's tragedy was for me an opportunity. I was asking them to open their home, hearts and life stories to me. In exchange for... what?

Instinctively I had huge respect for Lydia Khaba. I admired the fact that she had brought up seven children single-handedly and achieved her life's ambition at the same time. I thought her openness and strength in the face of her son's illness was remarkable. Not for her the shackles of stigma and shame that leads so many families to shun relatives with Aids. She urged her son to go public on his status. She tackled him on the contradictions between the safe-sex message he preached on the radio and his own reckless sexual behaviour. I was moved by the devotion she showed when he was in the miserable and humiliating throes of full-blown Aids. She changed his nappies, tended his bedsores, scrubbed his sheets and patiently endured his outbursts of fury and frustration. But I was increasingly perplexed by some aspects of her behaviour. At first, I put it down to miscommunication but later I began to think it was based on something more complex.

In the *Sunday Times* article which had apparently upset Mrs Khaba, I had written about his frantic struggle to find a cure for his illness and his increasingly desperate forays to *sangoma*s and faith healers and his antipathy to anti-retrovirals. I also wrote about his last desperate days in his mother's house in Emdeni. I wondered which parts of all this she had found offensive. There was only one way to find out. I called up Satch and we set off for Emdeni one Sunday afternoon.

Since my last visit, a pretty pink wall had been erected around the house. A tall gate stopped entry to the front garden. I remembered the neighbours and passersby popping in to greet Fana as he sat propped up in the winter sunshine and wondered how the new barriers could have been considered an improvement. Mrs Khaba came to unlock the gate to let us in and it was at once clear that she was very angry. Satch and I followed her to the kitchen and we all sat on stools around the breakfast counter.

Mrs Khaba said she had been very offended by my article. She hated the fact that I had said Fana consulted *sangoma*s when it was untrue; she hated the fact that I had quoted Sibongile; it was unseemly to have mentioned that Fana wore nappies and irrelevant to point out that Tine van der Maas was barefoot. "Must a nurse wear high heels!" she exclaimed angrily. I should have shown her the article before it went to print, she said. All other journalists she dealt with did so. Satch, who had been sitting on the stool opposite me looking distinctly uncomfortable, took the opportunity to make a hasty retreat, muttering about wanting to watch something on the TV in the lounge.

I took a deep breath. I apologised for upsetting her. It was the last thing I wanted to do when she was already so traumatised by her son's death. But I had made it quite clear when I visited the house and interviewed her that it was because I was writing an article. She had never asked me to show her the article before it went to print. I explained how I understood the larger significance of Fana's life history and how much his experience could help others. I said the example she had set as a mother who had embraced her HIV- positive child was a lesson to all. Mrs Khaba's fury evaporated. "It's like a cough when I'm cross," she said. "I just have to let it out." I was forgiven.

I said that I would like to interview her again as I was now writing a book on Fana. She agreed but said she must see the manuscript before it went to press. I remained silent, wondering how it would be possible to produce a book anywhere near approaching the truth if it had to be passed by someone who denied that he went to *sangoma*s and objected to my quoting the woman with whom he had shared his life for six years. However, Mrs Khaba seemed to take my silence as acquiescence and happily agreed to help me get access to the mothers of Fana's children. She wrote down my phone number and said she would get them to call me.

I was very troubled by this conversation. I couldn't get her to help me under false pretences. The more I thought about it, the more it seemed impossible that I could show her the manuscript. I needed to come up with another way of making sure that she also got something out of this. I thought back to my first meeting with the Khabas and Tsidi's question to me: "You are going to make money from this. What does Fana get out of it?"

Fana had been the breadwinner. His almost-destitute death would have deprived them of a crucial source of income. I understood from Sibongile that he had been supporting not only his children and their mothers, but also his mother, Tsidi and her children. Of the several hundred thousand rands Yfm had spent on Fana during the last year of his life, some R50 000 had gone directly to his dependents. There would also have been some royalties from his albums. But the money was unlikely to last long. Perhaps this was where I could be of help.

I went back to see Mrs Khaba in some trepidation. She greeted me warmly and we sat down in the small living room, which suddenly seemed much bigger without Fana's bed down the middle of it. I said it was unlikely that I would be able to show her the manuscript but what I could offer was a share of my profits in the book. I explained that this could well be a limited amount. Books did not make much money in this country, but it would be better than nothing. She seemed delighted with the offer and the question of prior approval of the manuscript instantly fell away. I asked her again if she could put me in touch with the mothers. She said that she saw the children all the time and promised to ask the mothers to get in touch with me. I left my phone number again and set off home with Satch. I told him about the new agreement and how relieved I was that the tension with Mrs Khaba had been resolved.

Over the next few weeks, every time my phone rang, I hoped it would be one of the mothers of Fana's children, phoning to set up an appointment. When nothing happened, I decided to visit Mrs Khaba again. Communication with the Khaba family was always difficult. Cell numbers I was given over the period I knew them seldom worked. So it was without an appointment that Satch and I pitched up at the Emdeni house on April 14, 2004. I mention the date because it was voting day. Exactly ten years had elapsed since democracy arrived and the ANC had taken over the governance of the country.

Fana's old school, Zwelithini Higher Primary School, had been commandeered for a voting station and a long queue had formed on the pavement opposite the Khabas' house. The voters showed the same good-natured patience that characterised the first democratic elections in 1994. They held up brightly coloured umbrellas to ward off the fierce autumn sun and laughed and gossiped as if they had all the time in the world. Hawkers had set up stalls on the pavement flogging snacks and an array of Tupperware containers of varying shapes and sizes.

Outside the sturdy new gate barricading the Khaba house sat a girl on a stool, chatting to a friend. I did a double-take. She was a female Fana, young and funky in black Nike sweatpants, T-shirt and baseball cap. She rose unsteadily from the stool to greet me, explaining that she had just come out of hospital where she had been treated for TB. She was Zanele, she said, Fana's youngest sister. I saw then that she was several pounds on the wrong side of slimness and there was a haggard glaze to the gaunt Khaba features. But she was friendly and hospitable, explaining that her mother was out on her *Watchtower* rounds but was expected home soon. She fetched a stool for me and we sat, companionably watching the voters opposite. Zanele said she did not intend to vote for the government because she had been living in a squatter camp in Lenasia for twelve years. "They're making all these promises because it's election time. But after ten years, I still have no house, no electricity."

Mrs Khaba walked up the road towards us and scolded Zanele for bringing the stools outside. They would get stolen, she said. But, nevertheless, took the stool I vacated for her. "It's my birthday," she said. "I'm seventy-five years old." Mrs Khaba explained that she had brought Zanele to live with her to ensure she took her TB medication and rested while she recovered. Later she intended to visit Zanele's home to ensure that Zanele's young daughter was properly equipped for her return to school. This was typical, I was to discover. She still automatically assumed responsibility for her children and grandchildren.

Meanwhile, the old lady settled down with us to watch the parade opposite. Mrs Khaba, it turned out, was also not voting for the ANC. Nor was she voting for anyone else on the list. "I voted for Jesus Christ," she explained.

For a seventy-five-year-old, Mrs Khaba was remarkably fit and healthy. Her only ailment, she said, was a little arthritis. All that walking around the neighbourhood flogging the *Watchtower* was clearly good for her physical, as well as her emotional, health.

I raised the question of the mothers. They had not contacted me, I said. Mrs Khaba said they were all busy but she promised she would get them to contact me soon.

I was at the time trying to understand the treatment Fana had received from the medical establishment. Mrs Khaba was convinced that it was during his ten-day stay in September at the Brenthurst Clinic in Parktown that her son first acquired the terrible bedsore that eventually ate through much of his lower back and buttocks. "They didn't accept that Fana came out of Brenthurst with that bedsore. But after Fana was discharged, when I wanted to change him, I found out that he's got this big bedsore. We had to take Fana back to Brenthurst and I had to speak with the matron there. They wouldn't admit – the nurses in ICU wouldn't admit – nobody admitted that they knew of the bedsore. I was sad. I was sad about the Brenthurst because they should be honest. But all they did was say I caused the bedsore. And nobody cared after that. I have never seen the size of a bedsore that Fana had in all my nursing career. It was so big, all big, huge, deep. But he never used to complain, you know.

"I went to the hospice at Mofolo and asked the sisters to come over to help me. And they showed me how to treat the bedsore. And then we got this other doctor. There's a new clinic here that the doctor took Fana to. He said Fana's wound won't heal because each time he passes urine, he makes number two, the bedsore gets wet. He said he must go to the clinic to change the system. They are going to put a tube in his bladder so that he can use a urine bag. And that was a very big operation. It took him five solid hours to do all that – to change the system, clean the wound, try to cut off all the dead skin around it so that it can heal." It never did heal. And a few weeks later, Fana died with the sore still eating away at his back.

I suggested to Mrs Khaba that we go together to the Brenthurst Clinic and ask to look at his medical records. She happily agreed. We made a date for the following week and I arranged for Satch to fetch Mrs Khaba at home and bring her to Parktown, where we met outside the clinic. I had arranged in advance for Fana's records to be made available and a secretary gave them to us and said we could peruse them in the boardroom. Fana's records were extensive: a great thick pile of loose sheets recording all the medication he received, as well as the nursing staff's two-hourly reports on his condition. A quick skim through the nursing records showed he was turned every two hours to prevent pressure sores. Each check concluded with the words 'Skin intact.'

We went back to the administrative centre and I asked if we could speak to the person in charge of nursing, Matron Sibongile Nchunu. After a while, we were led into the large office at the end of the corridor where Matron Nchunu was waiting for us. She was a beautiful, majestic woman with an air of command that slid rapidly into impatience as we explained our mission. There was a history here that I hadn't been privy to. Matron Nchunu started off politely enough, clearly constrained by the need to be courteous to an older woman, especially a bereaved one. But anger soon quickened and deepened her voice, and her breast heaved with barely suppressed fury. Mrs Khaba had been there before with another white woman and the same accusations, she said. She wasn't sure why they had to go over old ground again but she would do so if required.

"I sanctioned the ICU from home so that we would be able to see who was visiting him so he was nursed day and night. When the patient left, his back was examined. Three weeks after being discharged, it was claimed Khaba developed pressure sores while in this hospital." A few weeks later, she said, the Khabas brought Fana back to Brenthurst. "She insisted he be admitted here. They didn't want to pay because he had developed bedsores here. I said no way."

Mrs Khaba retorted, equally angrily: "When I took him home from here, I undressed him and saw his bedsore. I nursed for many years and I know what a bedsore is. It is bad nursing."

Matron Nchunu: "The man was pouring with diarrhoea! He was washed. My staff would have seen it [the bedsore]." Matron Nchunu said she understood that after Fana left Brenthurst, the Khaba family took him to a *sangoma*. That is probably where he developed the bedsore, she claimed.

This infuriated Mrs Khaba, who angrily denied that the family patronised *sangomas*. Now she was in a hurry to end the conversation. "We're not getting anywhere," she said. "Let's go."

I must say that I thought that the nurses at Brenthurst were models of compassion, particularly as regards Sibongile. The Khaba family had, somewhat cruelly, left her off the list of visitors required for patients in ICU. She told me: "They said it was because I was bringing my *muti*. The nurse in charge sat down with me and said: 'We know these things happen. It has happened to me also so we understand. They didn't write your name but we know who you are and we know your relationship with Fana and we are going to let you in. Just come when you want to come. Everybody in the ward knows you. You have the right to see him. Unless he tells us that he doesn't want to see you. But he has never said that.' And I did."

Later, I read carefully through all their nursing records. I saw no evidence of the neglect which could have led to bedsores.

From the Brenthurst, Mrs Khaba and I drove round to the vast public Johannesburg Hospital a few kilometres away and got lost in endless cavernous corridors before locating the records office tucked away in the basement. Johannesburg Hospital was Fana's final stop. I wanted to have a look at the records of his treatment and Mrs Khaba had agreed to give the necessary permission. Service was meticulous but unhurried until Mrs Khaba dropped her son's professional name. "Oh, Khabzela!" exclaimed the lady behind the desk excitedly and we got instant attention. They promised to have the records available a week later.

Satch took Mrs Khaba home and again, I waited for the mothers to call. After a few weeks, I realised that it was not going to happen. I was reluctant to bypass Mrs Khaba because, not only would this create tension between the two of us, but it might also put them in a difficult position. I knew that Mrs Khaba was a loving and supportive grandmother and therefore important to their children's welfare. I also knew that any funds available to the mothers and their children were funnelled through her.

On the other hand, Mrs Khaba had told me she was happy for me to interview them. She had even agreed to make this happen. And, in order to gain a properly rounded view of him, I felt I needed to understand what kind of father he had been. His children had been very important to him. Right to the end, he had insisted on including them in his life, despite the difficulties this had caused with Sibongile. And his relationship with the mothers had had important consequences for them, in some cases, fatal consequences. What was their attitude to him now? I knew that he had probably passed on the virus to at least one of them. How did they feel about this?

Reluctantly, I set about tracking the mothers down myself. Nonosi Mphela was fairly easy to find. She lived in Emdeni, a few streets away from the Khaba home. I went with Sizwe sama Yende, a colleague from Wits, and Phumlani Thwala, a young aspirant journalist who was helping with my research. Both were very taken with Nonosi and I could see why.

She had not been expecting us. We had turned up without an appointment, yet she greeted us warmly and took us into a small lounge with a couple of shabby armchairs. This was clearly not a well-off home. Nonosi was dressed in a large T-shirt and jeans, with funky, chin-length braids framing an elfin face. She was a shy, sweet-natured girl, clearly still in shock from Fana's death. A boy of about five sat entwined with her in the large armchair all the time we were there. He was the image of Fana and it was clear she was devoted to him.

Nonosi, now twenty-nine, was Fana's first real girlfriend and they were together for about five years. She remembered him as being "very shy". Their time together had mostly been spent in a domestic setting. "We listened to Radio Bop," she said. "We watched soccer on TV." But there were other girls, a fact that she, like Sibongile, just seemed to accept. "He was mad about girls," she said. "He had a lot of girls everywhere." Fana was driving taxis at this point and, later, working at Soweto Community Radio. In 1997 his family had paid half *lobola* for her, she said. They had agreed to pay the rest later but this never happened. Their son was born in 1998. On New Year's Eve of the year 2000, Fana had phoned her to say he had paid *lobola* for another girl and was going to marry her. The girl was Sibongile. Fana continued to visit his son and paid R500 a month child support. He also bought him new clothes twice a year. "I loved him so much," she whispered.

When Fana received the devastating news that he was HIV positive, one of the first people he phoned was Nonosi, while Sibongile sat in another room, nursing her own shock at the same news. "He said he knows he has hurt me so much. I must forget about it. He wants my support and love." Later, he visited her at home. "We sat in the car and we talked. He was telling me he loved me." When Fana came home to be nursed in his mother's home around the corner from her, Nonosi went to see him. "Going there and seeing how he suffered, I forgave him," she said.

Listening to Nonosi's faltering tale, I felt perplexed. Fana had phoned her and apologised because he needed support.

Did it occur to him that he had also put the fear of God into her, the woman who had born his child and had had sex with him for several years? Did he, finally, take responsibility for his actions? Or was his apology a catch-all for all the suffering he had inflicted on her, physical and emotional? It seemed unlikely because at the point of his discovery that he was positive, Fana still entertained the notion that he had been bewitched. His sexual behaviour would not have come into it.

But the possibility that he may have infected her is certainly haunting Nonosi. "The child has been tested and he's ok," she said. "But I'm still scared to take the test."

"Is it not better to know?" I asked.

She shrugged, looking down, somewhere deep inside herself. I felt desperately sorry for her. She seemed so trapped.

"What do you want for your son?" I asked.

"I want to get him away from here."

"Out of Soweto?"

"Out of the country."

Fana's death had deprived Nonosi of an important source of income. She worked as a waitress and her modest wage supported not only herself and her son, but also her mother and siblings, with whom she lived. The Khabas paid for the child's school fees, school clothes and his transport to school. "They say that next year there will be lots of money available." I listened to this with foreboding. I hoped they were not referring to the share of my royalties I'd promised. If it didn't amount to much, as I suspected, I feared there would be serious disappointment and blame might well need to be allocated.

A few days later, Phumlani went back to see Nonosi on some pretext or other and she told him the Khabas had told her off for talking to us. This confirmed my suspicion that I would have to persevere on my own. With Phumlani's help, I tracked down another of the mothers and her child, who was rumoured to be ill. We went around to her house and were told that she was at work. Phumlani went around later to try to arrange an interview and was told that the Khaba family had told them not to speak to us. He did, however, acquire a telephone number. We phoned a couple of times and the mother agreed to see us but without confirming a date. I offered to make up a false name for her and keep her identity private – apparently she had suffered from neighbourhood gossip about her health – but this game of cat and mouse continued for a while, with promises of meetings that never transpired. Eventually, I was forced to give up.

# N⁰ 9

After 1994, the fervour once channelled into politics went into partying. Years of youth lost to struggle were now reclaimed on the streets of Soweto in giant bashes that, in true democratic spirit, were open to all. Street bashes were organised by a small nucleus of people who printed flyers advertising where, when and at what time a bash was to be held. They'd put out a few chairs and lay on music. Partygoers would bring their own intoxicants – which usually meant beer and dagga.

These bashes played a cathartic role. Young people who, only a few years earlier, had been confined to their houses by police curfew between 10pm and 6am now partied the night away. Streets once colonised by Casspirs and police vans became giant dance floors. Spirits for so long cramped by fear and despair now exploded in collective celebration.

The street bashes were the perfect platform for Fana's nascent DJ-ing skills. Full Force offered its services and Fana soon became one of the most popular DJs at street bashes and was beginning to be well known around Soweto.

Kenny was not particularly enthusiastic about them. "The music would go on and on. Sometimes there would be fights when people were getting drunk. Some people would start shooting. I've seen people who tried to force girls into their cars during one of these street bashes. Gangs would come and disrupt them or there would be gang fights there. In the end these fights involved the police."

But it was from these bashes that the first new authentically South African sound in decades emerged. No one is quite sure where the name kwaito comes from. It could be from the word, *kwaai*, which means angry in Afrikaans, but in *iscamtho*, the township lingo made up of bastardised English, Afrikaans, isiZulu and Sesotho, *kwaai* means the edgy, dangerous side of cool. *Ou* is Afrikaans for bloke or guy. There was also a notorious Sowetan gang in the sixties and seventies known as the *amaKwaito*. *Iscamtho* is the language of kwaito lyrics, and gangster culture heavily influences its style.

University of KwaZulu-Natal musicologist, Christopher Ballantine, has written of how "No less a figure than South African President Thabo Mbeki urged the youth of his party to beware the 'distraction of kwaito'. Here's an example of the sort of self-regarding, anti-social and unashamedly sexist kwaito that Mbeki undoubtedly had in mind:

Translated excerpt from Thebe, *Bhek Indaba Zako* (Mind your own business):

*I screw girls*
*You get jealous of me*
*I go for cars*
*You say it's a Joburg style*
*I screw girls*
*You make me crazy*
*I'm just grooving*
*And you are looking at me*
*I control everything!"*

Everything about kwaito has deep township resonance. People initially danced to kwaito in the *toyi-toyi* style, which once would have signalled preparation for battle. Soundtracks include police sirens, gunshots and screams, stylised echoes of the terror of the previous decades, now hijacked by its previous victims and rendered harmless. One of the first big kwaito hits was 'Kaffir' by Arthur Mafokate. As in the use of Afrikaans in lyrics, the language and racist insults of the erstwhile oppressor were appropriated and subverted by those they once oppressed.

Kwaito is a sound of its time in that it is synthesised, relying heavily on new production technology. Like *iscamtho*, it is a hybrid sound which borrows from rural and urban, local and international to create a mix that is uniquely township post-1994. It includes American and European house tracks slowed down from 120 beats per minute to around 100; and elements of hip-hop borrowed from Afro-American culture mixed with traditional African sounds like maskanda. Gospel, jazz and classical music all figure somewhere in the mix.

Later kwaito songs express this same generation's yearning for a better life. Christopher Ballantine writes: "Leading singer M'du, for example, has a song that paints a bleak picture of crime and its consequences. Linked to the sounds of violent explosions, breaking glass and sirens, the song is a restrained monotonal chant, built over a dirge-like ground bass. Accompanied by a hint of a tolling bell, this dance moves almost like a funeral march:

A translated excerpt from M'du, *Bab ugovernment* (Father government):

*Father government! We are tired of stealing cars*
*Now is the time to stop this crime and live a normal life*
*Just like anybody else*

*Father government! We don't like being here behind bars*
*The boss is calling us: Six o clock! But we need to sleep*
*We like fighting*
*Life like this is not good*
*Friday afternoon, 12 o'clock, it's hot, hot*
*The brain is weak; I cannot think clearly*

*When I open the fridge, it's empty, only water inside*
*When the kids see me: 'We want bread!'*
*When my mother sees me: 'Go and look for a job!'*
*When my girlfriend sees me: 'You're useless!'"*

Kwaito was unique, emblematic; it was rocking the townships. But was anyone else listening? The short answer is no. The longer answer involves the exploration of a post-apartheid phenomenon, the grudging birth and startling growth of a radio station called Yfm. All this was a revelation to me. I had been to the odd kwaito concert in the staid halls of the South African High Commission in London when Cheryl Carolus, its most dynamic proprietor, was in charge of it. But by and large, I knew very little about kwaito or Yfm and the generation it had shaped and promoted: the Y generation, now so eagerly embraced by academics and advertisers alike. I also didn't know until I arrived back home and began my research into this generation that Dirk Hartford was so involved in its evolution. We arranged to meet at the Yfm offices so that I could catch up.

The Yfm offices are in the Rosebank Zone, the funkiest of Johannesburg's suburban malls and the one most popular with young people, black and white alike. Physically, The Zone was an appealing space; the escalators took me onto a broad, tiled boulevard flanked by shops selling global brands like Soviet, Nike and Polo. But there was also Stoned Cherrie, a post-apartheid South African label with its struggle retro style, Steve Biko's martyred image and 50s *Drum* magazine covers adorned T-shirts; traditional amaXhosa and amaZulu dresses and skirts rendered modern and funky with inventive beading and skilful cutting. As I walked, I was entertained by music videos screened on television sets suspended from the ceiling.

The boulevard opened out into a large, rectangular piazza, on the edges of which were branches of mall chain stores, Exclusive Books and CD Warehouse. But the bestsellers at this particular Exclusive Books were different from any other. They were not John Grisham or Dan Brown but Niq Mhlongo's *Dog Eat Dog*, a gritty tale about a boy from Soweto trying to hustle his way through Wits University; and Phaswane Mpe's *Welcome To Our Hillbrow*, about xenophobia and Aids in inner city Johannesburg. The Zone branch of CD Warehouse carried a prominent and exhaustive range of kwaito CDs as well as some of the best sounds from all over Africa.

Next to the CD Warehouse was the Yfm internet café and the Yshoppe, which led to the heart of the station, the Y studios, a slick, black-lined maze of sound-proofed booths. Through large windows, I could see DJs at work creating the Y sound at banks of sophisticated-looking equipment. The DJs themselves were young, glamorous, black-skinned and black-clad.

The Yfm offices are at the entrance to The Zone, almost opposite Stoned Cherrie. On the wall in the smart red and black reception hung a tableau of portraits of Yfm DJs: Fresh,

Bad Boy T, Sanza, and Monde. All smooth, even features and long, funky dreads. On the edge was Khabzela, with his dark skin, gaunt face, flappy ears and stubbly hair. I sat on the state-of-the-art cube-shaped red sofa and marvelled at the young people bustling in and out. If you listened to them with your eyes shut, you'd think they were middle-class white kids. They sounded and dressed exactly like my nieces and nephews. The only difference was in skin colour. It was so different from when I last lived here seventeen years ago. Black kids like this just didn't exist. It felt like a miracle to me.

Dirk came out to greet me and we repaired to a nearby Italian restaurant. I had barely seen Dirk in the twenty-five-odd years since we were at the University of Cape Town (UCT) together. We had moved in the same politically engaged circles – the white left, as we called ourselves – but, even then, I didn't know him particularly well. He was – and is – tall and good-looking, with the assurance and easy charm of old Cape money. His grandfather was chairman of Syfrets, the investment trust for the moneyed, and a chancellor of UCT. His godmother was Jane Relly, wife of Gavin Relly, a chairman of Anglo American. If he had followed the path set out for him by his family, Dirk would have ended up in the gilded corridors of corporate South Africa. How then did he end up championing successive waves of disempowered black people? Dirk, I discovered over the first of what turned out to be several glasses of wine, had begun his rebellion against his cloistered Wasp background well before we first met.

"My first real contact with black people on equal terms arose from the fact that I was a dagga smoker while at high school," he said. "There was absolutely no normal interaction between black and white in South Africa in the seventies – it was all master and servant stuff. Making my own connections with black people opened me up to a world which I found more and more I could empathise with, the deeper I got into it. Instead of going to the township just to score, I went to talk, to socialise, to smoke together. And I found I felt more comfortable there than I was at home.

"At the time I was going through a period of teenage rebellion and was rejected by my own community as a misfit. I was expelled from school and considered a source of terrible anxiety to my parents. But in the townships I was accepted. In fact, I have worked for and with black people my entire adult life and in all that time – nearly thirty years – I have never experienced even a hint of racism from black comrades or colleagues. On the contrary, I have always felt at home in black South Africa, much more than I ever did in the white world I grew up in."

After school, Dirk's father insisted he study for his undergraduate degree at the then very conservative and all-white Stellenbosch University where he again made friends in the surrounding townships. The 1976 uprisings "politicised these relationships overnight. By the time I left Stellenbosch University at the end of '76, having just turned twenty-one, I had been introduced to Mandela's speech from the dock at the Rivonia trial and the Freedom Charter. All I now wanted to do was work for the struggle, the ANC."

He went on to do honours at UCT, which was where our paths first crossed. "After UCT, I spent nearly three years in the UK – ostensibly studying for an MA but actually getting deeper and deeper into ultra-left revolutionary politics. By the time I came back to South Africa in 1981, my political loyalties were to the working-class movement which I believed would be the driving force of an inevitable socialist revolution in South Africa."

Back home, he worked briefly for the *Financial Mail* before joining the trade union movement, where he ended up as head of Congress of South African Trade Unions' media department in 1986. "Looking back on it, that period feels unreal – like a dream – because it was so hectic. I was detained during one of the states of emergency from our house in Mayfair when my daughter, Anna, was just five months old. There were petrol-bomb attacks on our house and our vehicles. Comrades were being arrested, tortured and killed."

I listened to him with a mixture of envy and admiration. I too had left university with a burning desire to fling myself into the struggle. I had become a journalist which, for me, essentially entailed being a propagandist for the liberation movement. But, after a few years, I was burnt out and exhausted. Democracy seemed an impossible dream. In 1985, I left for the calmer shores of Britain. I escaped those last, particularly fraught years of apartheid. But it also meant I missed out on the passion and intensity of those final battles and the euphoria that followed.

"The nineties, of course, were a whole new ball game," Dirk was saying. "The call came through from my comrades in Cosatu and the ANC to go and work for the SABC – the still completely intact mouthpiece of the apartheid state – to help transform the place from within. I was working with several old comrades in a new unit, the SABC strategic planning unit, and we were tasked with advising the new leadership on how to position itself as a public broadcaster in a democratic South Africa."

"The primary recommendation that we came up with was that a youth-oriented radio station should be launched on an existing national but essentially moribund channel called Radio 2000. We were still in political mode. The main driver for the idea of a youth station was the simple demographic that the overwhelming majority in the new democracy were young people and that there was little or no media directed at them. There was a radio station targeting white youth – SABC's 5fm – and very little else. The gap was wide open. We had a brand-new democracy where young people, in so far as they were given any attention at all, were written off by both the old and new establishment as a 'lost generation' who had sought liberation before education and were therefore uneducated and ungovernable; as a problem basically. No one was saying to young people – as we activists in the unions had said to workers in the eighties – that, come what may, we are on your side as we try to navigate this new country of ours. Although the concept was accepted in principle, not only by the SABC leadership of the time but also by the newly established regulator and the government, it was never given the go-ahead."

It was at the street bashes in Johannesburg's townships such as Soweto that Dirk first encountered kwaito. "We went out to have a look at what the youth were up to and it was mind-blowing. There'd be like thousands of people and lots of drink and zol and somebody with a hand-held mike and the sound cranked up to maximum. Even though some of the lyrics were limited to such glorious feats of wordsmithery as 'a pussy is a pussy', people were dancing in their thousands, chanting along. Some of the lyrics were a little more sophisticated than that but not very much.

"Kwaito was the first new, authentically South African music in decades and nobody was touching it. At the SABC it was unofficially banned because some of the lyrics were obscene and it was regarded as shit music. In the event, the new leadership at the SABC never had the courage – for reasons I still can't fathom – to give the go-ahead for a new youth station. By 1996, the new regulator, the Independent Broadcasting Association (IBA), announced it would entertain applications for several new commercial and community radio licences after an exhaustive examination of what was needed to protect the public broadcaster – in which we, ironically, had represented the SABC. Frustrated by the slow pace of change in the SABC and the lack of a decision on youth radio, I resigned." Unemployed now, Dirk and other former colleagues from the strategic planning unit set about applying for a commercial licence for a youth radio station. Yfm was the result.

The first hurdle was acquiring a licence. In their application, Yfm promised to fulfil certain rigorous empowerment criteria. Ownership would be 80% black; staff at least 50% female and, within three years, at least half the playlist would be South African music. It would be a multi-lingual urban station which informed, educated and entertained a young audience. The licence was granted – on condition that all these criteria were met.

The next hurdle was raising the money. Primary financial backing eventually came from the Union Housing Trust, the investment arm of the trade union-controlled listed company, Hoskens Consolidated Investments. Other shareholders were the Youth Development Trust, the Youth Investment Network, Mopani Media and Multi Media, all brand-new black-owned companies without money, assets or commercial experience.

It was only later, when I had spoken to local media experts, that I fully understood how difficult were the conditions under which Yfm was born. There was profound scepticism that youth radio for black people would work. The advertising industry was not only still white-dominated but entirely untransformed in its thinking. Despite accusations of racism, it persisted in refusing to recognise the potential of new, emerging markets.

Yfm initially set up shop in Bertrams, Hillbrow's equally insalubrious neighbour, in a building owned by the now-redundant voice of the ANC in exile, Radio Freedom, which was then ineffectually trying to reinvent itself as a radio station. "Against all expectations, including our own, Yfm became an instant and massive success," said Dirk.

"Because I was the main guy from the beginning, people think I had some kind of secret formula. But at the end of the day, the only message to the troops at Yfm was: we have this amazing opportunity. Most of you have never worked before – and most of our potential listeners are in the same boat. But we are now in a democracy and are free to be who we want to be and say what we want to say so let's reflect this. And that is exactly what happened."

Yfm staff at the time consisted of a tiny nucleus of mostly inexperienced, but very dedicated young people. Most of Yfm's original staff are still with them. They have grown with the station. Like Greg Maloka, to whom Dirk later introduced me.

It was Greg who played Yfm's very first track. "It gives me so much joy to say that," he recalled with a nostalgic smile. "It was Bongo Maffin's 'Makeba'." At thirty-one, Greg was general manager of Yfm. "I've done every job: ad trafficking; weekend DJ; music manager; program director; marketing and promotions; sales and events." A sturdy, quietly spoken man with a powerful physical presence, Greg in many ways exemplified Yfm. Born and brought up in Diepkloof, Soweto, he said his seven years with Yfm had been the best years of his life.

Sitting behind his desk in his bright, calm office, he recalled with wry satisfaction the negativity with which the birth of Yfm was greeted. "All the marketing and advertising fraternity, even the so-called radio gurus, told us everything about Yfm was totally wrong. Wrong target market, wrong format. They said the young black person had no disposable income. And essentially no future. We were all a bunch of hijackers. And the fact that we wanted to embrace kwaito! But because we were the target market, we understood what kwaito was capable of.

"In the two weeks that we tested our signal, I spent twenty-three hours a day playing that music. I brought 300 of my CDs and fifty from the station.

"I was looking at our crew, Dirk and all the other guys, through the glass in the studio and they were listening – actually listening – through a radio. Everyone just lost their minds. It was so exciting. We popped champagne at six in the morning and it was a really, really wonderful time. And now people wanted to get out and tell all their friends, which meant I had to keep playing the music. And we hadn't discussed how long we were going to test the signal for. For the next two weeks, I stayed on that spot, playing music for twenty-three hours and one hour resting.

"Towards the end of that two weeks, I really needed to get out, to see the sun, have a bath, change my clothes. I got out to drive to my mom's house and as I was driving through the intersection between Diepkloof extension and Diepkloof Zone 5, I could feel the sound getting louder. And I'm thinking to myself: hang on, my mother's little Honda doesn't have that kind of sound. So I turned the volume down and rolled down my window. And our music was blasting at me from everywhere, every car, every taxi. Two houses had speakers outside. It brought tears to my eyes. I just stood there and the light went green and red and yellow before I could move. People thought I was crazy or stuck or something. I just wanted to get out and say to them: this is Yfm. I'm the guy. I can tell you what the next song is. It was really a moment of pride for me, a moment of achievement.

"And we became incredibly popular. In taxis, for example. It was the perfect medium for taxis because drivers just want to have music on. And if you just felt like music, you tuned into Yfm. Everybody spoke about 99.2, the station that plays music only. It was quite a fresh thing at that point. And the music was really on the pulse; a touch of hip-hop, a touch of house, a touch of kwaito – really good stuff that people listen to and appreciate. That period was quite amazing for me. We were scared to get DJs because we thought we might ruin a good thing. Maybe we should just play the music."

At 6am on October 1, 1997, Yfm went live. "Beechies bubblegum was our first ad," said Greg. "They had the guts to buy the first spot. We started with the 6am news; played the ad and then we played 'Makeba' by Bongo Maffin. We started to introduce DJs and we were still received just as well because of where we positioned the station and we had begun to tackle serious issues that were on people's minds," said Greg. "Thank God, for a change, here is something that is about us."

Some 500 people applied to be DJs at Yfm. Again, they were recruited from the target market. Some were homeless, some were unemployed, most were untrained. But if they spoke to the audience, they were given a gig. Sixteen were finally chosen. Wednesday nights were open nights. Wannabe DJs would be invited to bring their tapes along and the best would be put on air. Wednesday nights, extra security was hired to cope because the crowds at the gate were so huge.

For Greg Maloka, Yfm was just another phase of the struggle. "For us, it was a revolution that had to happen, that had to be realised. It was this phenomenon that was for us and by us. We saw Yfm as another June 16, 1976 – just twenty-one years later.

"We became very involved in all the sub-cultures that were bubbling under. We held hands with kwaito when there was no programme director at any radio station that would be caught dead playing kwaito. We didn't care. We said these are youngsters like ourselves and this is what they want to hear. The one thing they need we have: a platform. And we're gonna give it to them. Within the first month, we had 600 000 listeners. And every six months, when the figures came out, they had doubled.

"We made kwaito and kwaito made us. All of a sudden, there were kwaito independent labels and a lot more people employed in the game of music. Businesses sprang up, like Arthur Mafokate's 999, Kalawa, TS Records and Hola Music. The music industry became stronger because we were playing it and eventually our competitors started to catch on. And all of a sudden, the youth market became significant."

One of Yfm's strengths was that, from the very beginning, they had a clear idea of who their market was. This was reflected in strong branding and a vivid logo: the large, solid red Y on a black background spelled out youth but it read as 'why?', a succinct and eloquent reflection of the questing, uncertain position of black urban youth at the turn of the century. Or, as Greg Maloka put it: "Before 1994, there was a common purpose. After 1994, it was every man for himself."

The marketing strategy was as innovative and risk-taking as the station itself. Initially, it relied on piracy marketing. Someone used to spray-paint the red Y on road signs so that it appeared all over town, in the most unexpected places. Stickers with the Yfm logo were stuck on every available surface. Some marketing tactics proved too much for the staid advertising fraternity. For instance, when Yfm sent round a fake Molotov cocktail to potential advertisers with the line 'This is what we used to do. Now we do radio.'

The tension between the money and the Yfm listenership – that is, the failure of the former to see the potential of the latter – remained a running theme. Yfm's listenership continued to grow but financially it stagnated. "They were scared to touch us," mused Dirk. "They said: 'These are just unemployed township youth. They have no money.' So, even though our audience numbers were soaring, our income remained static. Most advertising agencies were too terrified even to visit the station because of the area it was in. They thought they were going to get hijacked. I don't think it was really more dangerous than anywhere else but that was the perception. I'd hear all the time 'these Yfm people are fucking out of control.' People were scared of us because we appeared to be the voice of what were considered to be the 'ungovernable youth'. But they couldn't put us down because we had the listenership.

"The issues of global pop culture are all around sex, drugs and rock 'n' roll," said Dirk. "Yfm's first pamphlet read; 'Sex, drugs and kwaito.' What made Yfm unique was that there was real dialogue about real issues. Because the kids who were phoning in were not isolated cases. If they haven't been raped, they are having sex in all sorts of hectic ways. There's a lot of research to prove it. The majority of young girls' first experience of sex in South Africa isn't consensual. Most are forced into it. The whole youth culture is like that. If I tell you I like you, basically, it means I want to fuck you. You might be thirteen and giggle and try to get away but if you're at a gig and my *bras* are around, there's not much you can do about it. It's like being hunted down in a game park. The situation out there is horrific. We knew that. But how do you talk about these things? How do you introduce them in a way people can identify with?

"We did a show called Youth Crossfire for a long time. It discussed sexual issues and LoveLife sponsored it for a while. They would go out and find students at universities and high schools and the topic would be sex – safe sex or unsafe sex. It went on for two or three years in a very, very explicit format.... Insofar as we had an agenda, it was to raise consciousness around the issues of sex and encourage safe sex. Our view was that kids weren't talking to their parents about sex and vice versa. It's a taboo area. And our audience is young: sixteen to thirty-four, with an average of twenty-eight. Under-sixteens are not measured but we know we have a huge market in the teens. We were right in the middle of the Aids pandemic and we felt we had to do something about it.

"However, at the end of the day, we're also a business and we've got to sell our audience to the advertisers. We realised that what's cool for the listeners is not necessarily cool for the advertisers. So we had to repackage ourselves as these glossy, glamorous suburban people – which is also who we are of course – and not only as ghetto fabulous. Our listenership is not a homogenous mass. The funky babes on the covers of *Ymag* are who we are – but so are the unemployed youth living in shacks. With Aids, everyone is under threat, irrespective of race, gender and class, so the messaging on Aids remained the same."

The phenomenon of Khabzela proved just how strong the pull of the townships – and township identity – remained. Fana had a stint at Metro FM as a producer after he left Soweto Community Radio but he desperately wanted to be on air – on Yfm. It was towards the end of 1998, when Yfm was still in Bertrams, that Fana, armed with his demo tapes, managed to talk his way into the studios.

"One of our guys came to me and said 'Listen, there's this guy who's been working with Soweto Community Radio and he's really quite different – very funny – and he's desperate for a job at Yfm,'" remembered Dirk.

"We didn't have a space on air at that point but Fana had production skills so Greg suggested we put him behind the scenes, in production. It was pretty chaotic at that time and people were working day and night. Lots of people were doing production all night and then putting it on air the next day. Fana was immediately absorbed into this cauldron, working eighteen hours a day for the love of it. And later we said he could be on air a bit and we gave him a slot on Sunday and he just blew up. We only got audience listenership figures every six months at that stage but the first time we got them, he had the biggest audience at the station and it remained like that till he died."

The star DJ at Yfm when Fana arrived was Phat Joe, a suave, confident performer who went on to host his own TV show on both eTV and SABC1. Brought up in exile in the United States, Phat Joe spoke excellent English with a faint trans-Atlantic accent. When Phat Joe and Yfm parted ways shortly after Fana's arrival, Dirk decided to try the latter out in the prime breakfast slot.

"This shocked everybody because a) he was the complete opposite of Phat Joe, b) because he was a Johnny-come-lately to all the other DJs, most of whom had been there from the beginning and c) the breakfast show is the most important show on radio. It sets the tone for everything else. Within six months, he'd almost doubled Phat Joe's figures." Fana was wildly popular with everybody except the moneymen, the advertisers who were crucial to keeping the station afloat. Known as 'the DJ of the poor', Khabzela rapidly became a role model for a generation desperate for one.

For Phumlani Thwala, for instance, a twenty-five-year-old from Chaiwelo, Soweto, who lived in a corrugated-iron shack behind his mother's house. Phumlani dreamed of being a journalist and was helping me with my research, partly for the experience, partly for the pleasure of learning more about his idol. Phumlani's day job was packaging hair extensions for sale to black women who wanted flowing locks. He confided that, on bad days, when he thought he would never achieve his dream, Khabzela kept him going. "Every time you heard his voice, it brought hope. One would think that to be where he was, one of the best DJs in the country, one would have to have the best qualifications. But with only Grade ten, he managed to achieve his dream. Unlike the other DJs, he used the township lingo so that everyone could understand. And he addressed the youth about issues that concerned them, such as poverty, unemployment and relationships. He grew up in the township and his hard work earned him a suburb lifestyle and he ended up acting as a link between township youth and suburb youth. To me, Fana was an angel sent by God to the South African youth."

Greg Maloka was only too aware of this need for role models. "You know, apartheid has damaged people beyond imagination. The township has a vicious cycle. You've been in a really bad education system; your parents are in very inadequate jobs that can't provide for the family properly. You end up not having any opportunity. At some point you drop out of school, or you finish school and you can't afford to go to varsity. You try to make a living; you get caught sometimes with criminal elements. You start to drink. If you are a girl, you have a baby at a young age. And these days you get Aids and you die and that's the complete life of a person that finishes at around twenty or twenty-five. It's becoming really special to celebrate a fortieth birthday.

"Before Yfm, I felt myself to be in that vicious cycle. I started seeing things that are wrong as necessary and once you start to think that way… you know, stealing, crime becomes necessary because what else can I do? I can't go to school because I don't have money. I went looking for a job but no one would have me. You start looking at professional criminals.

"Growing up, we admired the gangsters. We aspired to be like them because, against all the odds, they lived their lives. They had money, they had cars. They had big houses. They didn't subject themselves to a system that had a glass ceiling. Unfortunately, we had fewer heroes in the corporate world and more heroes on the streets. So, it became extremely important to create a mindset that said 'this is not how things are supposed to be.' With Yfm, we were able to change that mindset. We were able to say 'hang on, guys, there is another way. Come with us. There's a whole lot of things on the other side of the tunnel you don't even know about.' We started Y-cares, our social responsibility branch, where we went out and found bursaries for deserving students. We tried to drive the entrepreneurial spirit, to start businesses like driving schools, car washes, spaza shops and shebeens.

"And Khabzela was at the forefront of that. We needed people like him who rose from the ashes to become an incredibly important person in society. He coined the phrase 'Positive Youth of Gauteng' to get people to think positively. He'd get people to call into his Sunday show to tell him what positive thing they had done that week that would allow them entrance to Positive Youth of Gauteng. And people would call and say: 'I used to hang with these guys and I realised that smoking and chilling and doing all sorts of funny things is not helping. So I've started my own spaza shop.' And Fana would say: 'Great. I'm going to support you. I'm going to come over there and buy from you.' And all of a sudden you had somebody who was so encouraging and so driven on your side. And you could tell people: 'I may only have a spaza shop but you get big shots like Khabzela coming to my spaza shop.' He knew the sort of effect that had on people and he shared it unselfishly.

"People felt the need to be part of Positive Youth of Gauteng. It was like being anointed. It became a really significant voice from the station. And it also resonated with those of us who had made it into the corporate world. We might be in boardrooms but we came from the same rough backgrounds. It attracted heavyweights in politics, heavyweights in business who rose from the same ashes.

"Another thing he did was to speak to people in prison on air. No one did that on radio. Prisoners would line up in jail to call him. They wanted to say hello to their families but another trend that developed out of the Positive Youth of Gauteng thing was that these prisoners started to call up and say: 'I really messed up. And to the youngsters out there: It's no fun in here − just so you know. I've wronged a lot of people. I come from this or that area and I really wanna apologise to those people. When I come out, I want to be a better man,'" said Greg. "You might say we shouldn't have allowed that because you give a bad reflection of who our audience is. But this was the reality of South Africa and we put our listeners before profits. And I think that helped us in that we reflected the reality of our audience. And Khabzela was extremely important from that perspective."

In 2002, in its bid to woo advertisers − and also to keep pace with the more affluent end of its listenership, who were all making the trek from township to suburb − Yfm moved to its current office in the Rosebank Zone. And Yfm is now an established and respected station, turning a healthy profit.

Kwaito has been absorbed into the mainstream, played by all the white stations. After gospel, it is the second biggest-selling music genre in the country and has created an entire industry in its wake. Kwaito stars like Mandoza and Kabelo are wheeled out for corporate and state functions.

And the Y generation is being courted by big business, as evidenced by a recent advert adorning Johannesburg billboards. The product was Hansa, Fana's favorite tipple. A good-looking young black man stared, confident and challenging into the camera. Alongside were the words in large type: 'I HATE BEING BLACK'. And, below: 'IF it means some people think that they know my criminal record. My rhythm. My level of education. Or the role affirmative action has played in my career. I'm not someone else's black. I'm my own. And I LOVE BEING BLACK.'

The DJ who came closest to filling Khabzela's shoes was his former technical producer, Ashifashabba. At the time I spoke to him, Ashifashabba had two four-hour slots on the weekends, from 10am to 2pm Saturday and Sunday, which incorporated the Positive Youth of Gauteng club. I caught up with him after his exuberant show one Saturday and found a surprisingly subdued man. He explained that, after a show: "I'm a sad guy. I feel like crying. I say to God: why did it have to be me? Why was I chosen?"

Shonisani Aubrey Muleya, the name given to him when he was born in rural Venda thirty years ago, had a spiritual bent. He was an Africanist with a self-imposed mission to promote African values. "I appreciate African culture," he said. "Like respecting the ancestors. They have you in their hearts. If you treat ancestors and elders good, blessings will come to you. And I believe there is witchcraft."

Like Fana, Shabba went to a township school, although his was in rural Venda. This set him apart from his colleagues. "Most DJs here are from white schools. We are colleagues at work but not necessarily friends out of work." He said he had no objections to black parents sending their children to school in the suburbs, as long as they encouraged them to retain their own language. African languages are crucial to the preservation of culture. As are jokes and folklore. Shabba created a career out of this, detaching himself from his brand in a slightly weird way, but nevertheless there was a sense of integrity and depth about him. He was genuinely ambitious – not merely for himself, but for his people and, indeed, his continent.

He developed a dialect he grandly called Shabba lingo, which combined Tshivenda, Sesotho, Setswana and Sepedi, an antidote to the isiZulu hegemony of *iscamtho* – and a deliberate rejection of English. He sometimes referred to himself in the third person, as in "Shabba was big. Everyone was talking about him and they wanted him on the show."

Like Fana, he grew up without a father, who abandoned his family when Shabba was a child. This was clearly still a source of pain. Unlike Fana, he shunned the party circuit and led a quiet, solitary life. "On Fridays and Saturdays, you'll find me at home alone, or with friends," he says. "Not at clubs."

Also unlike Fana, who believed he had a face for radio, Shabba had an increasingly successful TV career. He played the character Simon in the Tshivenda soapie, 'Muvhango', and also had a huge comedy show on TV, which was consciously African, in tone and content. "Presenters go on air to try to impress," he said. "Model C English is talking through the nose. People want to hear authentic African humour. Like the indigenous comedy *gooied* around the fire by the elders to entertain us but also to pass on messages to us. I tell the kind of jokes we share at shebeens, stadiums, weddings and parties." But the most serious thrust to his ideology is a vigorous rejection of global cultural imperialism. "We must not aspire to be American. We must not allow them to rape our resources. We can all be Africans. It's colour-blind. It's a state of mind."

Dirk has now left Yfm and Greg is in charge. Greg is quick to acknowledge his debt to Dirk. "Dirk is a wonderful human being. He has been really awesome for all of us, throughout all our careers at Y."

I thought there was a quiet heroism about white men like Dirk which was insufficiently acknowledged in the complex racial politics of the new-ish South Africa. He could easily have done what most of his white compatriots did on leaving UCT and exploited his privileged status for self-advancement. Instead he threw in his lot with the poor and powerless. Working with trade unions during apartheid meant a tiny pay packet and relentless state harassment. After 1994, he could, like many other white males, have whinged about affirmative action. Instead he diverted his considerable talents and drive into creating a new chapter in the narrative of post-liberation South Africa. And not only the staff at Yfm, but an entire generation of black youth gained a confident new voice on the back of it.

# № 10

The second millennium found Fana at his prime. He was the star at Yfm, the hottest radio station in town, presiding over the peak weekday drive-time show, as well as the iconic 'Positive Youth of Gauteng' on Sundays. He was the only DJ at Yfm working six days a week. The ugly, shy little boy whom everyone thought would amount to nothing – another township loser getting drunk whenever he could, abandoning girlfriends and children, getting by on petty crime – had taken on the various role models of his childhood and gone one better. Like the messianic preachers of the Kingdom Halls who had dominated his childhood, he inspired his followers with a vision of a better life. But, while the elders' influence was confined to the faithful of the Kingdom Halls, Fana had access to hundreds of thousands of people through his 'Positive Youth of Gauteng'. What's more, he had the intoxicating power of agency. The elders could promise a remote, hazy paradise sometime in the future. Fana could make it happen pretty well instantly by patronising the car washes and shebeens established by members of 'Positive Youth of Gauteng' and so hugely increase their popularity and profits.

There was lots of evidence that he was a giver. He wanted to help people and he did so whenever he could. Opposite Baragwanath Hospital, the biggest hospital in Africa, is the Takalani Home for the Disabled. It is a large, well-maintained institution, with manicured lawns and paved pathways tailored to wheelchair access. But inside its large airy dormitories were some of the most damaged specimens of humanity I have come across. I visited it one Sunday afternoon. The children were resting and all still in their cots. But the truth is that some never left them. There was a thirteen-year-old girl with the tiny, twisted body of a five year old. Children with huge heads, and missing limbs. Children permanently locked into a foetal position, with clenched and wasted arms and legs. One just shrieked intermittently – virtually all were dumb, many blind. They were clearly very well cared for but most had been abandoned by their families; rejects from Bara's maternity wards. After an hour, I was desperate to get out. It was all just too distressing.

Fana, the matron told me, visited the children twice a month for at least two years. He would perform for them at the home. Once he took sixty kids to the park. On another occasion, he organised for all of them to come to a show where he was DJ-ing.

"The children used to love him a lot," said the matron wistfully.

He was always available to help promote young aspirant musicians, making guest appearances on their music videos. His old teacher at Emdeni Junior High, Themba Ndlovu, said that when he was at Yfm, Fana would help raise funds for the school. "For instance, he would bring a music system to the school when we were hosting the Miss and Mr Emdeni. If he couldn't make it, he would send somebody to represent him and we could have his system for free. But later he would promise us that he was coming but he would not pitch up. It was disappointing."

Around this time, Fana became far more conscious of his image and, urged on by his friend, Kumza, he became interested in clothes. The scruffy township boy in his *mapantsula* clothes was transformed into stylish man about town. Fana now bought only imported Italian clothes from Hugo Boss and Versace, the smartest shops in the smartest suburban malls. He thought nothing of spending a couple of thousand rands on a pair of Italian shoes.

His cars became increasingly flash. Kenny, like several of his male friends, could rattle off a precise inventory of Fana's progression up the ladder of desirable cars. "Firstly, he bought a Fiat Uno, while he was working for Soweto Community Radio. Then he sold the Uno and bought a Sentra. And then he bought a BMW 528. And then he bought a BMW 328. And lastly he bought a BMW M3, which was faster than the 328. He had a passion for speed. He was a fast driver. But never once do I remember him being in an accident caused by him."

He was in an accident, though it does not seem to have been his fault. Sibongile recalled him running over and killing a child while they were speeding back from a club gig in Nelspruit one night. People came running to find out if he was alright because his name, Khabzela, was emblazoned across the back window of his BMW – he was driving a white one at the time – and he was famous, even out there in the sticks. Sibongile said the child had run out in front of the car. There was nothing Fana could have done to prevent the death. He did, though, pay for the child's funeral.

But Fana's greatest gift was the fact that he always took his community with him. As he rose, so did they. To this extent, he was a visionary leader. When he hit the big time at Yfm, Fana might well have done what countless other aspirant young black people had done and dropped the township as quickly as possible. Instead he took the township with him. The boy who had once been so proud of his English now spoke only the township dialect, *iscamtho*. All his references were township-related. He told township in-jokes, mocked his old headmaster at Emdeni High, conducted dialogues with taxi drivers and gangsters languishing in prison and focused his entrepreneurial exhortations on those quintessential township enterprises: car washes, spaza shops, roadside hair salons and shebeens. He flirted with women callers and boasted of his sexual conquests. Fana took the street corner – the clubhouse of township male youth – and put it on air.

Most importantly, he dwelled constantly on his own humble origins. He was forever reminding his listeners that he had grown up in one of the township's roughest corners, in poverty and he didn't even have a matric. And yet, "look at me now," he said. "So, however desperate you think things are, you can still be like me." It was this inspirational message that was so badly needed by township youth at the time, because they had no role models. Nothing in their upbringing had prepared them for life under democracy.

Barred from most skilled jobs, their parents had never learnt how to negotiate the upper echelons of corporate politics or to manage large amounts of money. And so they could not pass these on to their children. After 1994, black youth were catapulted into the wider world with few of the life skills needed to deal with it. Pressures on them were even more intense than on white youth because each black person employed to push up black numbers in lily-white companies had the weight of the entire community on his or her shoulders.

Fana showed them how to do it – and to do it on their own terms. He was very much a black man with a black man's culture. His message was: you don't have to give this up and play for white or Afro-American or anything else, in order to make it. You can be who you are and take pride in it.

And yet it was far from easy for him. Even at the height of his success, insecurity gnawed away at him. Greg Maloka saw it for himself. "He had a lot of insecurity. You would expect that. Here is a township boy who all of a sudden has to make huge decisions in the company. I went through that as well. There was a point where I was extremely insecure about the success the company was having. You ask yourself: can I play in this league? It's really hard work, asserting yourself and believing in yourself. It helps, having a supportive system. That's what we wanted to be for him.

"One of our competitors had a very strong 9am to 12am show so we needed a kick-ass show with someone who could draw the crowds. We moved him from the breakfast show and he was incredibly upset because the breakfast show is the most important. I sat him down and explained to him why we were doing it. And it dawned on him. 'So this means you depend on me?' he asked. And I said: 'Yes, we do.' He thought he had to beg us for everything. And I kept trying to drive it home to him. You are an extremely important individual and you can call the shots as long as you do it responsibly.

"And he strived for perfection all the time. He worked extremely hard to impress his audience, impress the company – to impress himself. He worked very hard to grow his brand and become a force to be reckoned with. And he did."

One of the ways in which Fana grew his brand was by making compilation albums which he would then promote on his show and in clubs. Mark Connor is head of Sheer Sounds, one of the independent production companies which sprung up around the indigenous music boom of the late nineties. He produced Fana's albums and, like almost everyone I interviewed, still intermittently gave way to grief while talking about him. Mark explained that DJs like Fana would go into a vinyl shop and pick tracks they liked. Sheer Sounds would then license the tracks and they'd be put out in a compilation under Fana's brand. Fana produced the Mekonko series – volumes one to three. Volume One sold 15 000; Volume Three sold 27 000; and Volume Two hit gold with 35 000 which, says Mark, was amazing for a Gauteng-based DJ. Only one track did Fana compose himself, the rest were international house. Fana was very passionate, even finicky about his compilations, getting involved in every part of the process, from selection to design to promotion.

"He was a very open personality. Cheeky, explosive and direct," said Mark. "He would come in with volume and leave with achievement. There were not too many dull moments when he was around. He pissed people off, made them laugh. Right till the end, he'd come in with new projects – when he'd have to be helped to walk. He'd say: 'I want to do this project with this artist.' And you knew it wasn't going to happen. He was still talking about new projects days before he died. But he followed his dreams and he succeeded, even if he died young."

Fana promoted his compilations on Yfm and on the club circuit. The latter involved an exhausting round of appearances that stretched from Mpumalanga to North West to Limpopo. For these sessions, he was paid around R4 000 a shot and he regularly made four appearances a weekend; sometimes it was four appearances a night. This, added to his Yfm salary of R28 000 a month, his 4% royalty on his compilation albums and his intermittent stints as MC and motivational speaker, must have earned him at least R100 000 a month. But, at his death, all he had to show for it was some sound equipment and a couple of BMWs. In the last couple of years before he died, Fana was rich for the first time in his life and he revelled in it, literally throwing money around.

In 2002, the year that Yfm made the move from grubby Bertrams to posh Rosebank, Fana and his fiancée, Sibongile, made the equally significant trek from his mother's house in Emdeni to Winchester Hills. Winchester Hills is on a ridge in southern Johannesburg, just a few kilometres away from Soweto. This move from township to suburb is a move most aspirational Sowetans make, with trepidation and constantly looking backwards, but it is an essential rite of passage. Greg Maloka described it thus: "Getting out of the township is going and finding yourself."

But it is really only a partial move. Most retain the family house in Soweto, where grandparents and other members of the extended family still live. They come back almost every weekend for weddings, funerals, birthdays, or for a night's *jol* at a shebeen or club. The township is where their circle of friends originates and where they feel most at home.

There is a common complaint that the suburbs are boring. People keep to themselves behind the high walls that surround most homes and they call the police if you try to hold a party. There is no street life. You sleep in the suburbs, they say, and live in the township. Soweto, by comparison, is still a huge village. Children play on the street; there are open-air hair salons on street corners, and groups of people sitting chatting under trees. Despite its origins as a racial ghetto servicing white Johannesburg, Soweto has developed a vibrant culture – and a strong sense of community. Most houses are open to the street and everything it offers. Everyone seems to know everyone else and they are constantly greeting each other.

Fana contributed generously towards the upkeep of the Khabas' Emdeni home, even after he had left. It remained an emotional base for him. It was to the Emdeni home that he returned when he was dying and, even now, his children regularly congregate there. For less successful members of the family, like Tsidi and her children, the Emdeni house remains a haven.

One day late in 2004, I picked Sibongile up from her father's home in Soweto and took her to Winchester Hills. She was looking neat and very feminine in a long, black and white dotted dress covered with a pale pink cardigan. The long braids attached to her hair were pulled back in a demure bun. She had had a bad cold and she still coughed intermittently and her voice was hoarse. This worried me, knowing how important it was for her to look after her health. But she insisted she was perfectly alright to make the trip and, indeed, was looking forward to it. Sibongile hadn't been back to Winchester Hills since she had lived there with Fana and her face glowed with nostalgia as we pulled up at the gatehouse to Phuket, the idiosyncratically named townhouse complex where they had first set up home.

The guard instantly recognised her, as did a woman chatting to him who turned out to have been their cleaner. They all greeted each other with rapture, hugging and enquiring after each other's health. As we drove inside, she showed me the townhouse where she and Fana had lived. The first thing that struck me about it was that this was about as close to township living as you could get outside of one. It consisted of rows of two-storey houses, some duplex, some single storey, separated only by cemented roads just wide enough for a car to pass through. All were surrounded by a high wall, and the only entrance and exit was via the gatehouse. The big difference from the township was in the view, which was spectacular. The complex was built on a ridge and, from the balcony of Fana and Sibongile's old home you could see for miles across the bare brown hills south of Johannesburg. I could see that their horizons from here would have appeared much wider, and that the sense of possibility would have outstripped anything the township had to offer.

But the sense of community was the same. Sibongile stood outside their old home and yelled at the top of her voice at the house opposite: "Didi!"

"This is what Fana used to do when he came home at night," she told me happily. "And they would stand here and talk for hours." Sure enough, within minutes, a woman in her mid-thirties emerged and, again there were rapturous hugs and exclamations of joy. Sibongile had not seen Didi since she left Phuket.

When the virus began to affect Fana's mobility early in 2003, they had to leave Phuket because he couldn't make it up the stairs to their second-storey flat. So they moved around the corner to another townhouse named after another Asian coastal paradise. Maldives was a much bigger complex than Phuket and was situated on a busy road. As Sibongile showed me around, I could see her becoming more subdued. "The day after we arrived here, he couldn't walk," she said, pointing out the ground-floor flat where they spent their last months together. She didn't like Maldives "because it's all black people," she said. "I prefer a racial mix like we had at Phuket because then there's control. There is no noise. People would put a note under your door if they were having a party."

Maldives was also where she had to contend with Fana's mother and sisters, who had moved in to look after him. She walked me to a little rock garden a few metres from their flat. "This is where I used to come and sit to get away from his family until I felt calm again."

# № 11

During the final years of his life, Fana spent a lot of time with three close friends: Satch, Doctor and Kumza. As with all his relationships, he seemed to feel the need to do something for them in order to retain their love and loyalty. His position at Yfm afforded him the perfect opportunity to do just this – and it had the added bonus of livening up his show. It fitted with his vision of reflecting the common man to include my friend, Satch; Kumza, a policeman; and Doctor, an events manager of sorts, on his Sunday show. They got to share his limelight – and all the pulling power and celebrity status that that entailed. So they chatted and teased and joked with each other and it all made for a highly entertaining hour with, for Fana's fans, the added edge of being privy to the intimate conversation of his innermost circle.

I met and interviewed all three of them but the one I knew best was Satch, my guide and companion on many of my trips to Soweto. At forty-seven, he was a good fifteen years older than the others. His age, plus the fact that he was dark-skinned and a Shangaan, made for a combination of social disadvantages that often rendered him the butt of the others' jokes. Not that he seemed to mind.

Satch, whose real name was Abel Hlaku, was Yfm's unofficial driver. He drove a *skoroskoro*, a wreck of a car that couldn't possibly have passed any roadworthy tests without considerable under-the-table inducements to the examiner. It frequently refused to start. The lights worked only erratically. It took me a while to master the complicated manoeuvre required to close the drooping passenger door. A smart lift and slam in one sure movement. The interior looked as if it had never been cleaned, the seats and floor were littered with rubbish and the aircon didn't work. Satch was invariably over-committed and was prone to being at least an hour late for appointments. Conversation was frequently interrupted by calls on his cell phone – most of which seemed to involve complex quarrels – and exuberant exchanges with drivers of passing cars and taxis. Yet I learnt more from him about life in Soweto than any official guide could have taught me.

Satch had intimate experience of township criminal culture and what it took to call yourself a man. From him I learnt that a sharpened Japanese-manufactured Allen key (British or American made ones weren't as good) was best for breaking into cars, and that it was possible to slide under a car and disconnect the alarm in the owner's garage and get it out without waking him. He conceded though that this was a while ago – in his wild youth – and his tricks probably wouldn't have survived the advance of security technology.

One day a few weeks after I first met him, we had a meal at Rosebank's Nino's restaurant (my treat and strictly business). With his cell phone out of service and no diversions apart from a cold beer and a thick rump steak, we finally had an uninterrupted conversation.

Satch's life in Soweto began in 1964 when his father, a policeman, brought the seven-year-old Satch and his mother from their home in rural Limpopo and dumped them with his cousin in Mofolo, Soweto. Hlaku senior then disappeared. Some years later, he was badly injured in a stabbing incident and returned home so that his wife could take care of him. "He couldn't move; he couldn't cook; he couldn't do anything for himself so he was forced to come back to stay with my mother. That's when I started to know my father."

Hlaku used his clout as a policeman to get his family their own house in Meadowlands. Three more children were born. "Then my mother started seeing that things were not working out with my father, so her brother gave her money and she started a small business selling bananas and apples on the road. Then she started to sell chickens. She employed about thirty people to chop chickens and take out their feathers. Life was good because we managed to go to school."

His father, meanwhile, absconded for weeks at a time, usually with other women. "My mother was from the bundu and guys in the townships believe that if you are from the bundu, you don't have TV; you are not up with the style of living: you don't know how to kiss a man. My father was learning new skills here: how to treat a woman, how to take a woman to a movie, a restaurant. With our mother, it was different."

Satch was soon well on his way to a life of delinquency. "I was so naughty. I was not doing my homework, not attending school. I would tell a teacher where to get off because I thought I was too clever." He left school without matriculating and embarked on a life of petty crime, strongly influenced by the need to prove himself a man. "When you are still young, you are forced to do things that you are not supposed to do, or they will never consider you as a man when you grow up. Like stealing cars; hijacking. You must first start stealing from your place. You can steal anything that shows your manhood; that shows that even outside, you can make it on your own without your parents looking after you.

So I started stealing from my mother. She was selling chickens. I stole live chickens, gave some to my girlfriend, sold some and it started right there. And because stealing was in my system, even when I worked at a company I was stealing like that company belonged to my father or to me. I just took things. I could steal a whole truckful of products."

His mother, he said, was constantly bailing him out. "She was always paying money for the bad things I did.

"Usually I did it because I just wanted to prove to these guys that I can also be a man. I am not a woman because only women cannot go there and do these things. So if you are a man who cannot do such things they used to call you Sophie or Jane – ladies' names – and say: 'Hi Sophie, you don't have a liver' [you are a coward]. They would say: 'Hey *laaitie, kom hierso*' and they would send you to go and do something, like go to Sandton to fetch a match. And if you are weak, you will do that for the rest of your life."

In the 1970s, a new industry was born which was hailed as a shining example of both free-market enterprise and black empowerment. Over the next three decades, the minibus taxi industry became the main form of transport for urban black commuters. Costing a few rands per trip, minibus taxis were quick, regular and efficient. They were also frequently dirty, in very poor shape and dangerous – especially if you happened to get caught up in one of the frequent territorial disputes between rival taxi magnates.

In 1983, Satch was such a magnate. Owner of fourteen minibus taxis, he was riding high. "I was so rich. From 1986 to 1990, I was one of the youngest people in Soweto to drive a BMW 325. But because of jealousy, this *isidliso* came into my life and took everything I had until I was down on my knees.

"This *isidliso* is like a black magic thing. They can put a snake in your stomach. Or a frog. A moveable thing that can control your life. With that *isidliso* inside your stomach, it can take your money and give it to the person who gave you that *isidliso*. You can't understand how it is happening. You get bad luck for the rest of your life. You can be rich and you'll fall down. You can be a good writer, and nobody will buy your book. You can be a runner, and no one will pick you to represent your country.

"Sometimes you pay the witch to bewitch someone. Or someone can bewitch you, like your family or your wife. This *isidliso* is mostly given by wives to their husbands because they want to hold us. You must belong to her only.

"I went to my *sangoma* and he told me about this *isidliso* in my stomach and the person who put it there and the reason for that. It was my aunt and her children because I was too close with my aunt's children so they had the power to do that. We eat together, sleep together; do everything together. They took my clothes, my underwear, my socks – everything that can hold my sweat. They went to this *sangoma*. After going there, they managed to get, what do you call it, this small thing that eats grass, that has short horns. It is like a cat – a cat-size thing that leaps. They killed it and after killing it they took everything out and they wrapped up everything, all my things, and they went to a grave and put it in a grave. When the taxi war started, I became the first to be targeted because of the *isidliso* my aunt put in me.

"Those Zulus will never be happy until they see you underground. They targeted my drivers because I was in hiding. I slept in a different place every night. Most of my drivers were killed. But God and my ancestors were with me.

My enemies would see me and start shivering and I'd vanish from them. By 1990, I was left with one car. I sold my roadworthy certificates for next to nothing. I was bankrupt. I had to start my life again.

"I looked at my wife as if she was a piece of shit. She stank. If I started beating her up, she will run away and I will live a single life. She went to her mother. I loved her so much but this *isidliso* made me beat her up and chase her away. I was very depressed. I nearly committed suicide. I thought: what is the good of living?

"It's like having a baby inside you. You can feel the baby turning. But I'm a man. I can't be pregnant. A hospital can't see it. I went to a doctor to be checked and there was nothing. You have to go to these *sangoma*s. Some *sangoma*s would never tell you the truth. They always lie to you. I spent R14 000 on these *sangoma*s till I got the right one. There's this good *sangoma* in Soweto. He could see the problem I am having with this *isidliso*. You drink a lot of water with medicine inside. It shakes the *isidliso*. It is big and can't come out through your throat. It can jam and you can't breathe and you can die. Most people die. It either goes out through trumpeting [vomiting] or downstairs. Mine came out in pieces but you could see it was a snake. I got rid of it four years ago. Now I've got a house and three cars. People have started loving me again. Now my aunt's children are scared of me. They are now thinking I am the witch."

I suggested to Satch that there might have been a different explanation for his troubles. He was one victim in a general taxi war over control of routes. Possibly he was picked on first for tribal reasons. He was Shangaan and the taxi industry was dominated by Zulus. The loss of his business and his fortune sent him into a depression and he took his anger and frustration out on the person closest to him: his wife. It need not have been an *isidliso*. He listened politely and then resumed his story. Quite clearly he thought I didn't know what the hell I was talking about.

Before we parted, Satch undertook to arrange meetings with the other two members of the inner circle, Kumza and Doctor. But, without Fana, it seemed it was much more difficult to assemble the old gang. Two meetings were set up and, at the last moment, one or other of the two dropped out. Satch phoned me in exasperation the second time. "Kumza's wife says he has been out all night. He is still living in the old way."

But eventually we managed to meet. The venue was a makeshift bar beside a petrol station in Daveyton, the township adjoining Benoni, where Kumza lived. Doctor arrived first and we bought beers in a little café next to the station and settled down on plastic chairs arranged under a lean-to outside.

Doctor Malabi was a surprise. A tall, good-looking, pale-skinned man, his manner was quiet and contemplative and his command of English excellent. He was very different from the shambolic, emotional Satch.

He told me that he was born in Hammanskraal thirty-one years ago and had graduated from Wits Technikon with a qualification in management accountancy. There followed a job with Medscheme but "as I went along, I realised that being an employee is not my thing. I'm more on the giving instruction side. I think I might do better if I get into something of my own.

"Whilst I was still working for Medscheme, I started a company called Mamepe Promotions. I think we emerged in

125

1999. I used to do gigs at tertiary institutions, organising orientation parties and so forth and I engaged a lot of guys who were then DJ-ing. That's when I met Fana. I introduced myself to him. I think it was in early 1999. I used him at one of our promotions. Viva, you know, it's a mixture of Red Bull and vodka. From then, I made sure that at all my parties, all my gigs, my events, I used him. Sometimes it was as an MC and at the same time as DJ.

"I believed in him. He was not popular at all and I decided I needed to have one or two guys that I could always rely on. The business was still very young and we could always negotiate. I'd say to him: 'my man, we didn't do well here; we didn't make a lot of money'. He would understand and say: 'Don't worry. We'll do another one and if it goes well, you can give me whatever you want to.' So we started that kind of relationship. And, then in 2000, when he was doing his weekend slots at Yfm, I would go there and when we made some money, I would go and give it to him there. That is how I started meeting the other guys.

"When Satch used to come through, we thought, he is not our age group. Probably he wouldn't like what we're doing. I just ignored him until it happened that we ended up being friends. And then Fana came up with the idea of Positive Youth of Gauteng. And he said: 'Why don't we formalise this; have a sort of club that would be registered? If you are a Positive Youth of Gauteng, you need to affiliate to the club; become a member.' We said: 'Look we've got different expertise. I'm from the marketing side; Satch is from the transport side; Kumza is from the police side. Why don't we combine all our expertise?' We started working on that. Unfortunately, it didn't kick-start as we planned because we all had our other commitments. But at a later stage, he continued with it on air every weekend.

"By then he was starting to be recognised. Actually he was already there, you know. Wherever he was going to perform, we used to accompany him. Wherever he was performing, we were there, supporting him. We would hire a microbus and go there, all of us, in the microbus. After each compilation album that he recorded, there would be a tour, a national tour, at tertiary institutions, at clubs across the country and if he drove, he would take us along. If he was supposed to fly, he would go there on his own.

"He could do three performances in one night. I remember once he started in Rustenburg and after Rustenburg he had to perform at Nelspruit. He left Rustenburg at about nine and got to Nelspruit at around three-ish in the morning. And then he had to perform, you know. After that he would refresh and come back to Joburg around eleven the next morning. He was so dedicated. He loved what he did. But sometimes he would look exhausted. Really exhausted.

"And every day our friendship grew. We used to meet mostly on weekends. We used to share our feelings and everyone knew each other very well. We used to park our cars at one place. He would pick us up and we'd use one car wherever we wanted to go. Not The Zone or Sandton City. No, he was uncomfortable with that. It was never his style. But at the township, we used to braai meat and buy *pap* and eat. I used to know only part of Soweto but since we were together, I knew almost 70 to 80% of Soweto. Wherever he went, they knew his car. Every third or fifth minute, someone would be hooting. I couldn't believe it. The entire township, corner to corner. Particularly the taxi guys. He would give them a cassette, one of his compilations and they would get excited."

A sour note briefly entered the relationship when, in 2002, Doctor finally gave up his day job at Medscheme. He felt the gang did not give him the support he needed. "I started to have a number of problems there [at Medscheme]. They would see me as a threat. I decided you know what: let me just call it quits." He resolved to devote himself full-time to Mamepe Promotions. "I could say I battled; starting a company from scratch. It was really difficult. But I told myself: I just need to be patient. If you start a business of your own, you need to market yourself. Wherever you go, network. These other guys, that's one thing they didn't understand. They always asked me: what are you actually doing?" And then Fana, the gang's leader, began to falter.

"Early in 2003, one of the guys I used to work with closely in business was shot. He used to live in Orlando. About a month after that, Fana started to be a bit sick. He couldn't walk properly. We asked ourselves what might be the problem. But we couldn't understand. The following weekend, when we got together, he decided to tell us. He said he was HIV positive. We were all shocked. We couldn't believe it. It was a very sad experience for all of us. And we said: you know what? He needs our full support. He was deteriorating and by then I was not that busy and I decided to dedicate most of my time to him, to take him to Yfm and back home. Because by then he was no longer able to drive himself.

"The last week of April and the month of May I did absolutely nothing but concentrate on him, making sure that he's taken wherever he needs to go; take him into the loo and so forth. Still all of us were there as friends. Whenever we could, we used to go to his house and sit around with him. But it was really difficult. It was my first experience to be close to a person who was HIV positive, particularly one who was starting to be sick. Somewhere along the line we had a big misunderstanding with the family. We heard him say 'Hey guys, come whenever you want to come; come with your drinks; come with your beer; please come and enjoy yourselves'. He didn't want us to just sit and say: 'hey, my man. You're sick, you know.' No, he wanted everything to be normal. And they couldn't understand that.

"Most of his listeners knew all of us and wherever we were going, everyone was asking: 'How is he? How is he doing?' We were keeping them posted. Obviously we can't just say: 'He's getting worse.' And on his birthday, September 12, they really expected something. Like, it's his birthday: what's going on? We decided to do a party for him. At a pub in the township itself. The yard is quite spacious. It's got lawns. The guy said: 'You can use my venue. I want to be part of this thing.' We thought Fana would be better. We could try and bring him over. But unfortunately he was bad. We decided we're not supposed to stress him by trying to pick him up. It wouldn't be a good idea. We decided to carry on in his absence. Everyone understood he won't be coming to the party. It went well. The yard was packed to capacity.

"Even now I dream of him. I dream of him getting better, standing up and saying: 'Look, I can dance.' We all miss him so much. When I try to come to terms with his death, I say to myself: that's how the Almighty wanted it to be. He took him from nowhere and made him someone. He just wanted us to learn from him."

Doctor got up and wandered sadly off to join Satch, who was buying meat in a butchery over the road. Kumza meanwhile had finally arrived – in an official police vehicle – and, after collecting a beer for himself, sat down beside me.

Kumza Nkosi, it turned out, was an inspector who had been in the police force for fourteen years, based in Benoni. He was resplendent in full uniform, complete with gun on hip. Then thirty-four, he was married, with three children. Large, confident, oozing bonhomie, even in this time of mourning, there was an air of mischief about him. Unlike the ascetic-looking Doctor, one got the impression that Kumza savoured the good things in life and expected them to be at his disposal.

Kumza's first encounter with Fana was with his voice. He heard him on Yfm shortly after Fana began working there and called him up. "I said: 'You're a funny guy. I want to meet you.'" Shortly afterwards, Fana did a gig at Club Stamina in Benoni, Kumza's stamping ground, and they met in person. "He gave me a T-shirt and a sporty. We exchanged numbers. He said: 'I want you on my show.' He said I must co-present."

An intense friendship ensued. "He used to phone me three times a day, like a woman, to tell me he loved me. His sister, Tsidi, said we were gays he used to call me so many times. Even our friends used to complain that we give each other so much attention. We used to be like close, very close. For me he was tight. He was a charmer. His voice would touch anyone. His voice would destroy any woman. Khabzela was not handsome but women were chasing him up and down. He would say: 'I look like a chimpanzee. But hey man. Women love a man like me. I drive a nice car.' But there was one person who wanted to destroy his life. I think it was a woman."

Fana also dressed very well and Kumza took the credit. "He was the best dresser and he took that from me. I asked him:

'Khabzela, you're an old-fashioned guy from Zola. You wear these funny *mapantsula* clothes. But now, my brother, you've changed. Look, you're driving a beemer; you're staying in the southern suburbs. You're tight. You have to change your clothes.' He said to me he doesn't care about clothes. But one day he phoned me and told me: 'Kumza, I've changed my mind. As a breakfast DJ, I need to look sharp. What can I do?' He changed his *mapantsula* clothes to good and expensive ones, only Italian. He used to say when he was drunk: 'I speak, dance, dress Italian.' He used to be proud of that. All Italian clothes. Only Italian.

"But sometimes, he would fight with me. Khabzela had two sides: his soft side and his hard side. If he doesn't want something, he doesn't want it. If he wants it, he will tell you.

"He was like a father to me, and a brother. I used to love him. 'Focus,' he used to say to me. 'Focus. Make everything count, every woman count. Achieve your goal. Don't let failure overtake you.' Those were his words: 'Don't let failure overtake you.' But he was open-hearted. So warm in his heart. We would meet here and he would buy everything: food, beer, whatever and we'd have fun. Since he died, no one's doing that. I don't think I will have another friend like Khabzela. I'm not yet ready to go back to Yfm. I want to mourn Khabzela's death until I know I'm fine. I'm healed. Then I'll go back. There are so many things to say but some of the things are very sensitive. I can't talk about them here because his family would be very much hurt." Overcome by all this talk about his dead friend, Kumza said, choking: "I'm getting emotional now." We got up and went to look for Satch and Doctor. On the way, Kumza said contemplatively: "As a black man, Khabzela did something wrong so God and the ancestors withdrew their protection."

We found the others at a makeshift braai in an empty field behind the butchery. Delicious smells wafted from a steaming pile of boerewors and chops beside the fire. The men were standing around drinking Amstels and munching meat, together for the first time since Fana died and they all looked appropriately solemn. I had to confess to a moment of scepticism. I wondered what they missed the most – the man, or what he did for them. Their world must have seemed a much duller place now they could no longer bask in his reflected glory. Excepting for my good friend, Satch, of course. I am sure his grief was genuine.

I asked Sibongile about the trio. Her attitude to them was perhaps coloured by the amount of time Fana spent with them when he could have been with her and the fact that much of their bonding was over other women. But she did not doubt the intensity of their friendship. "Kumza and Doctor are the two people who know Fana more than anyone," she said. "Especially Kumza. He's the person who knows Fana best. There was a time when they were very angry with him because he was talking out all their secrets. What they were doing, with who, when. Fana was telling them that they are supposed to tell their wives. He's tired of keeping secrets.

"They used to pick up women together," said Sibongile. "They went to these hotels together. I used to find hotel slips. I don't sniff around people's things. I would see maybe a Holiday Inn slip and just throw it away. I didn't care. But then it came up: 'Remember that woman you used to take to the hotel. What was it like. Huh?' At that point I didn't care because I knew everything already. They always felt, Fana, you can't say those things in front of Sibongile. And he'll be like:

'It's done; the damage is done already. What am I hiding?' But if he wasn't there, they were not going anywhere. He always paid for everything. He paid, he paid, he paid."

Later Satch told me that he'd tried to persuade the friends to go for an HIV test. "There is one woman who was chowed by Khabzela and now she is being chowed by Kumza, which I couldn't understand. I spoke to him about that and it was like, 'I am okay. I know myself. Don't worry.' I said: 'Okay guys, let's go and test, all of us at the same place.' They wouldn't go with me." Satch said that he didn't sleep around because he had his eyes on the road. "I did maybe drive them from point A to point B. I was going to these places because I was driving only for Yfm at the time but when they started doing their thing with chicks and the like, I drove home."

Nevertheless, he said he was so traumatised by what happened to Fana, that he went twice for testing at Joburg Hospital. "They checked and I'm still negative and I said 'Thanks God'."

Six months after my meeting with Doctor and Kumza, the latter went to a party held by celebrity kwaito group Mafikozolo and got blind drunk before climbing into his car to drive home. He drove at high speed through a red light, smashed into another car and was killed instantly. That Sunday, Satch was on Yfm, mourning the death of the second of the foursome. He said lugubriously: "Khabzela is calling each of us, one by one."

# № 12

It is safe to say that Fana Khaba was fantastically promiscuous. Fana himself was entirely open, not to say boastful, about his exuberant sex life. When I had lunch with him six months before he died, he told me he had frequently had three women queuing up outside his bedroom door to have sex with him. There was an unashamed, if slightly unhinged, tone to his other boast to me: "I drive around Soweto and look at all these women with their HIV-positive children and think: they're all mine. Mine and God's."

His official partners seemed to have accepted the fact that they were not only the women in his life. Nonosi Mphela, for instance, said that while she was going out with him: "He had a lot of girls everywhere. He was mad about girls." Sleeping with the same women was part of his bonding mechanism with his close friends. Said Satch: "There is one woman who was chowed by Khabzela. Now she is being chowed by Kumza."

When he became a celebrity, the temptations − and the pressures on him to perform − snowballed. Satch claimed there were sometimes five girls a night. "These kids would say, like: 'I don't want to be loved by Khabzela. I just want him to fuck me.' And when that thing happened, it's like a trend. You know: 'Khabzela fucked me so nice'. So, like, all the places he went to, they used to talk about that. And the others, they would want to have a taste of that too."

The erotic appeal of the celebrity is not peculiar to South Africa. All over the world groupies line up to have sex with rock stars, footballers, chat-show hosts − whoever fills the celebrity slot in that particular culture. The problem is the local variation has worse consequences than accidental pregnancies or sexually transmitted diseases that can be cured with a shot of penicillin.

Fana Khaba accumulated both during his sexual marathons. He had at least five children by five different women – none of them by his fiancée, Sibongile – and he suffered from regular sexually transmitted infections. But at some point, he also acquired HIV – and passed it on. He passed it on to Sibongile and also to at least one of the mothers of his children. Mpho Mhlongo told me about her. "One child and one mother are sick," he said. "The child is two years and she looks very frail. You can tell she's sick."

Then there is the woman whose furious missive on the Yfm website struck a jarring note amongst all the outpourings of love and grief: "I waz one of his girlfriends! Damn on me 4 cheating on my boyfriend; now I am also dying."

But I thought Fana's notion of masculinity might also have created a fault line. Who were his role models? His father, Petros Khaba, was a troubled soul, to say the least. His brief, turbulent presence in Fana's life must have left a deep impression – but so would his much longer absence. Greg Maloka said: "He was very angry with his father. He missed him and he wanted to prove to him that he could make something of his life. He always had a need for a father."

The substitute male role models provided by his mother would have been the elders in the Jehovah's Witness church. They would have represented the extreme end of the moral spectrum: chaste, non-drinking, imbued with religious certainty. At the Jehovah's Witness meeting I attended in

Chaiwelo, one of the erect, dark-suited elders read out the following chapter from Corinthians 5:11:

"Do you not know that unrighteous persons will not inherit God's kingdom? Neither fornicators nor idolators, nor adulterers, nor greedy persons, nor drunkards will inherit God's Kingdom. Every other sin that a man may commit is outside his body but he that practises fornication is sinning against his own body."

I wondered if flashbacks like these from Fana's childhood might have had some impact. In the end, his behaviour was profoundly self-destructive. Was he, at some level, inviting retribution? And, at the end, did shame and fear of divine disapproval exacerbate his anguish – and contribute to his erratic behaviour?

Jehovah's Witnesses are very conservative socially. A man is the head of the family; the woman is there to serve God and her husband, in that order, and bring up the children. Any sexual activity outside monogamous marriage is forbidden. Looking around the Chaiwelo Kingdom Hall, it was obvious that most of the congregants were single mothers. Forbidden an active sex life, it seems reasonable to assume that large amounts of sublimated eroticism were directed towards the male elders on the stage. In *Watchtower*, most of the pictures of those who had been saved, who were within whistling distance of God's Kingdom, were white. This too might have influenced Fana's – and Mrs Khaba's - susceptibility to white miracle-peddlars when he was dying and desperate.

The other male role models in Fana's childhood represented the opposite end of the spectrum: the hard-drinking, womanising gangsters who dominated street culture. He tried to amalgamate these two warring male icons. As he got older and was trying to free himself from his mother's apron strings, he became more receptive to the gangsters. The sub-cultures he most closely identified with were those dominated by marginalised, macho males: taxi drivers and prisoners, many of whom were from the Sowetan gangs he grew up with.

The theme of his intervention was an almost biblical redemption. Prisoners were encouraged to confess and apologise on 'Positive Youth of Gauteng'; the community to forgive and embrace them. I wondered if this attitude too came courtesy of the church elders. *Watchtower* of August 1, 2004 quoted Mark 10 and Luke 7: 'Never did he assume a superior attitude towards those whom he served or cause them to feel inferior. People of all sorts – men, women and children; the rich, the poor and the powerful, as well as noted sinners – felt at ease with him.'

In Fana's company, the sinners probably felt even more at ease, given that he did a fair amount of sinning himself. Not heavy-duty gangster sinning like burglary, hijacking or murder. But when it came to a materialistic lifestyle and predatory sexuality, Fana was up there with the best of them. On air, Fana regularly boasted of his conquests. He referred to his penis as his 'anaconda' and made regular reference to its activities. As in "my anaconda ate last night" or "my anaconda is hungry."

Kenny Ndaba spoke scathingly of this culture. "They call them playboys. They show off with this girl and next week it's another one. It is to boost your ego. And the girls go with them because they have a flashy car. The girl wants to be seen in that car, to show her friends: 'Look, I'm driving in a BMW.' She doesn't try to find out if that guy has other girlfriends as long as she can brag to other girls. It is very competitive and it has got worse since 1994 because a lot of people can afford it. That's the reason we have such a big number of people with HIV."

As Kenny pointed out, the cost of this lifestyle is high – and not only in terms of one's health. Sexual favours are often exchanged only in return for some material reward. A major drain on Fana's income, according to Sibongile, was the money he spent on girlfriends. "You support these girls," she said. "They expect you to be loaded. They want money, they want clothes."

One of Soweto's post '94 landmarks was a nightclub called The Rock. It borrowed its name from the area in which it was situated, Rockville, one of more salubrious bits of Soweto. Nearby was Moroka Park, a green haven of rippling waterways, children's swings and vast, shady willow trees. The Rock had ochre-coloured walls, deep couches and a curved aluminium bar with a six-inch deep iced groove in which you could keep your beer cool while perched on one of its high stools. A winding staircase took you up to a vast terrace from which you had a bird's eye view of the surrounding terrain. This included the parking lot opposite, on the other side of which was Panyaza's Butchery, The Meating Place for Quality Braais. The parking lot was invariably full of extremely expensive cars. There were Porshes, four by fours, and lots of BMWs. Over at The Meating Place, men sat around on plastic chairs while chops and wors grilled slowly over makeshift braais.

Twenty-seven-year-old Vuyo Mabuno was a Rock regular and knew most of the other regulars. The posh cars in the parking lot belonged, he said, to men who had made it out of

Soweto, who now owned fancy houses in the white suburbs. But the suburbs were where they went to sleep. Soweto was still their spiritual home. Mostly they were middle-aged men who left their wives and girlfriends at home. "They will tell their wife or girlfriend they're going to the car wash," said Vuyo. "But what car wash takes eight hours? This place attracts a lot of eye candy. The girls' average age is about twenty-three. You see eight of them sitting together in skimpy clothes. They are looking for a guy with a car who can buy them drinks and give them a lift home."

Fana used to come to The Rock and Vuyo spoke about him with the same near-adoration as most young Sowetans. But he was also deeply conscious of the perils of the celebrity culture to which he believed Fana fell prey. He told an anecdote about a top Yfm DJ who was due to play at The Rock one night in the winter of 2004. "There were three drop-dead gorgeous young girls who were trying to get in but they were told it was full. They said [the Yfm DJ] had invited them. Half an hour later he arrived and brought them in with him. They chilled together all night and then all three of them left with him.

"When these DJs play in clubs, managers are at their beck and call because they know DJs are a crowd-puller. DJs are hot property because they run a tab and the girls get free drinks and get in for free. And I'll perform a favour or two for him in return.

"When Khabzela played at The Rock, there was a stampede," said Vuyo. "You would take a girl to a club and you'd go home without her. She'd have gone off with the DJ. She can brag to her friends: 'I slept with Khabzela.' They're living for now. They want to be seen with the in crowd."

Kenny himself believed that there was also a deeper, personal reason for Fana's promiscuity. He thought it was rooted in the sexual humiliation he endured as a teenager. "When we were growing up, he thought he was ugly. He felt rejected as a young man. No girls were interested in him. At church, in school, in the street. He used to propose [love] to girls at church but none of them was interested."

Fana's teacher, Mr Ndlovu, saw the same pattern: "They [Fana and his group] would always tease the girls. But you could see they didn't know anything about girls. You would hear them saying: 'Hey, *mina ngathatha iviki lonke*' [Hey, I can take you to my place for a whole week]. But when they left it would be without girls. They weren't taken seriously. I remember they would say to the girls: '*Ngashaya* eighteen rounds [I can take you for eighteen rounds of love-making]. And the girls would just reply: 'You are young boys. You don't know what you are talking about. You have not experienced it yet.' But they were not seriously into girls. The girls in turn enjoyed their company, their jokes, because they knew they were safe around them, unlike with the other boys."

Said Kenny: "When he got famous, he took it as payback time – payback to all those who teased him for the way he looked; for being a 'Watchtower'. On radio, he used to say: 'You may think I'm ugly but look at the girls I'm going round with. Look at the car I'm driving.'"

Kenny believed Fana's relationship with Sibongile was always doomed because he was not ready to settle down – and he might never have been ready to do so. "He was not the marrying type. He was pushed into paying *lobola* for Sibongile. His mother wanted him to have a stable relationship because she knew that he had many girlfriends.

But having paid *lobola* didn't keep him at home. I think the reason for that was because of his job. Girls used to throw themselves at him. And that was his downfall."

There is another warning in *Watchtower* that might have played on Fana's mind when he was dying and demented: 'There are numerous bible examples showing that the world's view of greatness leads to ruin. Haman's craving for glory led to his humiliation and death. What about haughty Nebuchadnezzar, who was stricken with madness at the height of his power?'

I sometimes wonder what Fana would have been like if he had lived to forty or fifty, the age when, if we're lucky, we slough off the conditioning by parents and society and decide for ourselves who we truly are and truly want to be. I wonder what sort of man he would have become. Because, God knows, it was pretty hard to fashion a decent sense of manhood out of the examples set out for him. He seemed to me essentially a fragile creature, deeply dependent on women and their approval. The picture that emerges of Fana's world does not reflect the traditional South African stereotype of women as victims, men as brutes. The women seem to have had a strong sense of themselves and their needs while the men danced around them, trying desperately to meet these needs, fearful all the while of their own pointlessness if they failed to do so.

# № 13

Fana first began to feel ill early in 2003. "It was in about February or March," recalled Sibongile. "He started complaining that he was tired most of the time. There was a day when he came home and said: 'Sweetie, my legs are wonky.'

"And I didn't understand. I said, '*Ag*, it's your Hansa.' Because he loved his Hansa. He drank it every day. We never thought HIV. We all never thought HIV."

Fana himself thought he had been bewitched. So did his friend, Satch. Satch thought that Fana had fallen prey to the same curse he himself had fought so long and hard to exorcise just a few years before. Satch believed Fana was being eaten up from inside by an *isidliso* in the form of a snake.

"Even the way he walked was like a snake," recalled Satch, making torturous sideways movements to illustrate his point. "And we started running around to *sangoma*s to find out, to get him something to eat or wash or burn. Maybe if it was a snake, it would go away and he could start his life again."

Sibongile, who did not believe in witchcraft, was sceptical: "The *sangoma* said someone at Yfm wanted to kill him because he was jealous of him. The *sangoma* even told him who it was. And he believed it. And if you believe in something, things will happen to confirm it. If someone looked at him a certain way, he would conclude certain things from it. He started taking this *sangoma*'s *muti*."

But it didn't help. At Yfm, it was becoming increasingly clear that Fana was in trouble.

He was taking more and more days off work. There were rumours that he was falling asleep in the studio. In March 2003, *The Star* carried a horrific story about a fifteen-year-old domestic worker who was allegedly forced by her employers to have sex with a dog. Fana immediately and erroneously assumed that the employers were Afrikaans. He said on air: *"Afrikaners, asseblief, kaffirs is nog mens, jy weet. Moenie dink want ek is swart en then ek is a vark. Ek is ook mens."* ("Afrikaners, please, kaffirs are also people, you know. Don't think that because I am black I am a pig. I am also a person.")

As it turned out, the alleged perpetrators were not Afrikaans at all. They were Taiwanese. An Afrikaans man named Mr T Labuschagne heard the broadcast and filed a complaint of hate speech with the Broadcasting Complaints Commission of South Africa on the basis that Fana's words had caused him and other Afrikaners extreme distress. Fana and Dirk immediately apologised to Mr Labuschagne but Yfm was found guilty of hate speech. On appeal the verdict was reduced to one of unfair and untrue comment but Dirk and Greg were appalled by the association of hate speech with the station and Fana was warned that if it happened again, he would be taken off air.

Dirk said that, in retrospect, Fana's powers of reasoning had already been affected by the virus. "He was probably already partially demented." Although Dirk and others at Yfm suspected Aids, Fana's own reluctance to face up to it made it difficult to engage him directly.

"At Y, we have tried to create a very free culture," said Dirk. "You can talk about anything. There is no dress code. No one comes down on you if you are late – just as long as your work overall is being done properly. Conversely, no one would even think of asking for overtime pay. Most people work all hours of the day and night because they want to.

"From the very beginning Aids was a big issue for us because it was a big issue for our listeners. We didn't have millions of education and training sessions but we did create a space for it to be discussed internally and our on-air people grappled admirably with it on an almost daily basis. But when Aids struck us directly, it felt as if we had never discussed it. It was so hard to deal with. You see someone displaying all the signs of the virus but it doesn't make it any easier to raise it. The thought that Fana might be HIV positive crossed my mind several months before I actually spoke to him about it. But even while I was thinking about ways to approach him on the issue, he was coming to me with stories about how he had been bewitched by a fellow Yfm staffer as an explanation for why he couldn't come to work every day and demanding we investigate.

"He said he'd been to doctors and there was nothing wrong with him," said Dirk. "He said there was a stone in his penis. He said he'd had radical sexually transmitted infections at one stage. So the signs were there but we still hadn't engaged him on the issue. He was so awkward about it. The bottom line is it's very hard to raise the issue of HIV directly with someone who is in complete denial."

Greg Maloka was in Durban at the time. "Fana called me and said: 'I'm really upset because there is a rumour going around that I have Aids and I don't have Aids.' Now we had already debated this. A lot of us had seen the symptoms before but you don't just walk up to your friend and colleague and say: 'Are you positive?' But now that he had broached it himself, we could deal with it. I cut short my trip to Durban because I could sense that he felt very alone and I know what he's like when he's in that space. He doesn't like being in that space."

One day soon afterwards, Fana had to be carried in to work, up in the lift from the underground car park, past the Primi Piatti restaurant full of early morning coffee drinkers and into the Yfm studio. Later, Dirk walked past the studio and found him asleep on the floor in the corner while his co-presenter, Dreshne Pillay, struggled to carry the show on her own. Dirk went over to him and gently shook his shoulder: "I said: '*Bru*, we need to talk.'"

Together Dirk and Greg helped him to a table in an adjacent restaurant. "We suggested he be tested for HIV and I'll never forget the look of relief that passed over his face," said Dirk. "It was as if he'd been waiting for us to say it. He said: 'Okay. I'll go this afternoon.'"

Satch took Fana and Sibongile to Baragwanath Hospital for their tests.

Sibongile described what happened next. "They gave us pre-counselling. This woman was sitting there talking to us and I was sitting next to the window. People were passing up and down, going on with their lives. Just before they brought back the results, I said to Fana: 'Look at me' and he looked at me and I could see tears in his eyes. He never thought it could happen to him.

"And this woman comes in and she asks us: 'Do you want me to give the results to both of you together or do you want to be in separate rooms?' So I say: 'I would rather have mine alone.' And he goes out and she comes in, holding this paper. Believe me, when you've never been to that room, you can't say anything. It's like a dream; someone will wake you up. This woman says to me: 'Do you want me to read the result to you

or do you want to read it yourself?' I was like, 'Just tell me! I just want to know.' And she says: 'You're HIV positive.' And then I cried. I cried and cried. I think I stayed an hour crying inside that room. And then I looked outside and just looking at those people walking up and down gave me the strength to say: 'You leave this room and you join them. You go on with your life, no matter what.'

"But when I went outside, Fana was standing there. I couldn't look at him. I didn't hate him but I was angry. Look, I'm just human, I was angry. But the main thing was I just wanted to come home. I wanted to tell my parents and my sisters. I didn't want to hide it. I wanted to tell everyone, every single one."

The next day, Fana broke the news of his status to Greg and Dirk. "We said to him: 'You have a choice,'" said Greg. "'Either you deal with this thing quietly by yourself but the downside of that is that there are all these rumours out there and you know they greatly affect you. We will have to say you are ill and people will draw their own conclusions. On the other hand, if you decide to come out, we will support you in whatever way we can. But it will also be incredibly difficult to deal with because of all the stigma around Aids.

"'That's your choice. You go home and think about it. But as soon as possible you need to get into a programme because we need you back at work.' I remember the first thing he asked was: 'What about my job?' I said: 'What about your job?' And he said: 'I cannot lose my job!' And we said to him: 'We love what you do. You are a very important asset to the company. The fact that you are HIV positive means nothing. It just means that you've fallen ill and you need to get better.' He was so happy about that."

Said Dirk: "If Fana had refused to come out publicly about his status, we would have had to accept it. But the minute he did, we had to deal with it. We gave him a day to tell his family. He called a family meeting. They gave him their blessing. He came back and recorded a message about his condition and we played it that day, over and over again."

That was April 16, 2003. The response from the Yfm audience was instant and overwhelming. Thousands of emotional fans jammed Yfm phone lines and chat boards with messages of love and support. The following are just a small sample:

'*Hola Khabzela baba*. We are all saddened by what has happened. You are a big asset to our nation. Wish all the high profile peoples in our country can disclose their status like you.'

'having hiv doesn't make u less of the great person u are but disclosing it makes u an even greater person!'

'by revealing your status you have already beaten this virus. We are with you all the way brother. I hope other people can be as brave as you have been.'

'Khaba, you are my role model. Without you on air I'm nothing. Plse be strong. You're one of God's sweetest angels.'

'BIG UP to you, Khaba. *Winja sbali*! It took a lot of courage to do what you did. Be strong, *mfana* and remember you have the youth of Gauteng on your side. I love you, Fana, you've made such a difference to my life. Now it is your turn to get support. WE LOVE YOU.'

'Just know that the public is one hundred and one percent behind you. You hve already made a statement – I decided to get tested today! Thanks for giving me the courage. I only realised now how real HIV/Aids is. Live on Khaba!'

'Khaba, look on the positive side. You have the support of

Y management, the youth of Gauteng, your family and friends. Unlike others who are less fortunate, they discover their positive status, lose their spouse, lose their jobs; can't afford medication and get rejected by their OWN families. So, whenever you are feeling low, just remember you are 1 of the VERY fortunate few.'

This last fan was, of course, entirely correct. Devastating as Fana's news was, there were few others in the country in as good a position from which to fight the virus.

His family was right behind him, so were his fans. And so was Yfm. Even though Khabzela was an independent contractor at Yfm and was not on a medical aid scheme, the station assured him they would continue to pay his salary, all his medical expenses and keep his slot open until he was well enough to come back. Meanwhile, he was to go home, begin his anti-retroviral treatment and, if he felt up to it, record his progress in an audio diary. Yfm hoped to become the first broadcaster in the country to host a regular show on living positively with Aids with a presenter who was himself HIV positive. In the meantime, Dre would present their show on her own. "Certainly, once we'd made him the promise, we had to stick to it, come what may," says Dirk.

The impact on advertisers was mixed. "If, as some do, they think our whole audience is going to die of Aids, then Fana simply confirmed this. But, on the positive side, if they didn't believe it before, hopefully now they can see that we're not just party people. We are, above all, responsible and caring people."

It was at this point that Fana made a decision that transformed his life from one that was a huge and valiant success against all the odds to one that was a tragedy.

"In retrospect, we were naive," said Dirk Hartford. "We thought he'd take his ARVs and be back at work in a few weeks. And then he'd become a fantastic icon for living positively with HIV."

The best course of action for Fana – and the one Dirk assumed he would follow – would have been to remain quietly at home, not drinking alcohol, eating healthily, resting and avoiding stress. He would have had to swallow his anti-retroviral pills and endure the side effects which, for the first fortnight at least, are often very unpleasant.

Looking back at where he had come from, one can see why this might have been difficult for him. The man who had fought so hard for power and control over his own life would have had to give it up. Acknowledging how ill he was and submitting to the treatment required to make him well would have required a temporary surrender of his independence, a reversion to an infantile state.

I was at the time taking out a little boy from an orphanage a couple of times a month. He was born with HIV and spent the first years of his life in a hospice, almost permanently ill. At the age of two, he was put on ARVs and, by the time I met him a year later, he was, apart from a seemingly permanent cold and regular bouts of diarrhoea, a cheerful, healthy little boy.

Aids is difficult to manage in children. Their immature immune systems are constantly battered by colds, flu and any other bugs doing the rounds. Their viral loads are thus very difficult to control, but anti-retroviral treatment is still very effective in boosting their immune systems sufficiently to ward off serious illnesses.

At first I was daunted by the battery of medicines I had to pour into his mouth twice a day – no fewer than three liquid preparations in precise amounts: 3 mls of this; 6 mls of that; 10 mls of that. And I couldn't make a mistake. These were powerful drugs. He had to take them at exactly the same time every morning and every evening and I had to make sure he ate first. There had to be food in his stomach to help him tolerate the drugs. But I soon got used to it because he was so compliant. He'd eat whatever I fed him and happily swallow whatever liquid I put into his mouth. If only Fana had behaved like this, I thought. But then he would have had to revert to childish submissiveness, and childhood was not a place Fana would happily have revisited.

Fana did take ARVs – for a while. "It was in his mind that ARVs would kill him," said Sibongile. "He took them for a week and then he started taking *sangoma*'s medicine. I guess at some point he just got desperate and took whatever people said would cure him."

But it is also possible that Fana, emasculated and humiliated by his weakness; in terror at the prospect of losing his job at Yfm, the source of so much of his hard-won self-esteem, was flattered by this new wave of courtiers. Once again, there were people fawning over him. He had power. He could make a healer famous by trying out his or her cure.

Greg was visiting Fana at home regularly, and his eyes filled with tears as he described the disaster he witnessed unfolding before him. "I'd see him almost every day. I'd feel bad if I couldn't go to see him because he always felt the need to talk to me, just to make sure things are still fine. He kept saying: 'Am I still going back to the show?' And I said: 'Yes, Dre is still doing the show by herself. We haven't put anyone else in there.' And one day he was worse; the next day he was better and when he was better, he would just talk about the things he wanted to do when he came back on the show. You know, how he's been listening to the show and they're completely fucking it up and he wants to come back and sort it all out. It became incredibly difficult to deal with."

By all accounts, the situation in the Maldives flat was desperate and chaotic. Fana at this point had chronic diarrhoea and could hardly walk. His mother and sisters had moved in to help nurse him so the little flat was packed with fraught women. His beloved BMW stood abandoned outside the flat. His feet could no longer work the pedals, a blow for a man whose car was an extension of his ego. Sibongile was in a state of shock. Not only did she have to deal with the news of her own positive status but also the revelation of the extent of Fana's womanising.

"I guess I forgave him when we left that hospital, because I had to," she said. "I had to do it for myself. But when we went through counselling together and things started coming out – horrible things, things that no one could bear, believe me – I was looking at this man and thinking: 'I don't know you.' He was saying he slept with such and such and so and so. And the babies started coming up, the children that he'd had with other women. When I met him he had three. So now, he had another two. I hear there are others. I was sitting there thinking 'I am going to die. I am going to collapse and die.' I couldn't take it. I had to deal with the fact that I'm HIV positive. I had to deal with the fact that my husband was sleeping with other women in my house. The fact that there were children involved was like cutting through my heart with a sharp knife.

"The saddest part was that the people he had children with were people I knew. People who were close to me, who were looking at me every day and smiling at me. And I even knew the kids. At one point, I went to Woolworths to buy things for a child, not knowing it was Fana's child. We both took the things to the woman's place, with me not knowing that it was his child.

"The other one stayed at Winchester [the same townhouse complex at Winchester Hills]. At some point when she was pregnant, my instinct told me it was Fana's child. I told Fana: 'I know it's your child.' And he denied it. He denied it! This girl knew he had a wife. She saw me every day with Fana but she went on doing whatever she wanted to do with him. Because, you see, I never went with Fana to these parties. I would always stay at home. So these girls would go with him and that's where they did their stuff. And then he would come back home.

"There were tears every day. Little things were coming up every day. Fana has done this. Fana has done that. Fana has another baby. And I was expected to deal with them every day. And Fana would leave the house and go see those children. We are trying to sort our relationship out here but he would just go and see them and their mothers. And I was expected to sit in the house and swallow it.

"What made me more angry with him and his family was that they expected me to deal with everything. There was a point when the children were brought into the house while I was here and they were just saying: 'Sibongile, deal with it.' No one was feeling the pain I was going through. No one was saying: 'Sibongile, we understand and appreciate what you've been doing.'

"For me, it was worse because I didn't have a child. I don't know why. I just didn't fall pregnant. I believe it was God's plan. Because if I did it would be a mess. The child would be sick and I would have to be spending money taking the child to doctors. He came up with the excuse that he had other children because I couldn't have children with him. He said that and his family said it too. What did I expect him to do? I couldn't give him children so he had to get them somewhere. You can imagine the pain that caused; them saying that now I have to accept these children because I can't have children.

I asked: "So you knew he was unfaithful but you didn't realise the extent of it till after you found out you had HIV?" She replied: "Sometimes, when you're in a relationship you try not to see things. Then people come and tell you stuff and you find stuff but you still ignore it because you love this person and you want to make it right. There was a time when we fought a lot and I didn't know why we were fighting. There was just confusion. When we fought, he would bring me here [to my father's house]. And when I went back to the house, I would find a sign there was a woman there. You see how women are. You think you are the owner of the house but we are many. So she will always leave something, like an earring. I would always find things like that. But he would come up with excuses, like his friend was here with his girlfriend or whatever. I knew that he was sleeping around but I hoped and wished and prayed that he was using a condom. I would tell him: do your thing but please use a condom. Do it for me, if not for anyone else. And he would just say: '*Ag* no. Why do I need to? I'm not sleeping around.'

"But still, still, you know, I wanted to make it work. There was a day when he didn't know I was coming. A woman had left five minutes before I got there. She left my key with the security guy. The guy told me: 'There was a woman who left the key here. Was it your sister?' People were looking at me with that shamed look, saying 'if only you knew what was going on.' A friend of mine was staying in the same complex. Our houses were opposite each other but he didn't care. My friend told me: 'I'm sorry if you're going to hate me for this but what is going on is totally out of control. He is just way too much now.'"

Most of these revelations came out during counselling sessions with Masi Makhalemele and Angie Diale of Tsa-Botsogo, a non-governmental organisation (NGO) which helped people living with HIV. Masi was recommended to Dirk by the Gauteng Aids Unit after he appealed to them for help in dealing with Fana. Both Masi and Angie were themselves HIV positive. Their experience with Fana clearly made a deep impression on them but the most lasting is one of frustration. After six months with the family, they decided to withdraw, convinced there was nothing else they could do.

Masi said that they "dropped everything for Fana. The first time I walked into his house, he swore at me. He was so rude. He didn't want to listen. If he would just have listened, he'd have been okay. This was an angry man. It was as if there was something black inside his heart. He had a look back at where he came from and he hated what he saw. He knew he had done so much wrong. He had infected so many girls. Sibongile kept shoving the paper [saying she was positive] under his nose."

Masi and Angie said one of Fana's fatal flaws was his inability just to sit still, to come to terms with the enormity of what had happened to him and realise that, for the first time in his life, he had to relinquish control. "He felt: 'I can't lose this now.' Everyone wanted to please Fana. He came from a culture of male dominance and here were all these women telling him what to do. He couldn't go to the toilet by himself. He had to be bathed. And this was a hero! It was all about controlling women: they can't live without him. It was such a dysfunctional family."

His hyperactivity, which had helped him get where he was, was now a hindrance. "Fana was constantly on the phone. All these people were coming in and out. Taxi drivers, DJs, boozers. They'd walk into the house and he would try to be a hero."

Some visitors were helpful: "Mdu Masilele came. He was brilliant. He understood everything. Zola sat there and held his hands. He brought him rosaries. Mandoza came and the young people from Boom Shaka. But most had their own agenda. Some of them said: 'I slept with a girl you slept with.' All these doctors, traditional healers – all wanted a piece of him. They knew they could become famous through him."

But, at the very end, when he lay dying in Johannesburg Hospital, the stream of visitors had almost dried up. Yfm DJ Andile Gaelesiwe, who visited him frequently, said that Fana felt that some of his closest friends had abandoned him. She attributed their absence to fear: "I think his illness might have reflected what they will go through in the future," she said.

# № 14

Dirk said that even with the wisdom of hindsight, it was difficult to explain why Fana spun so badly out of control once he left the Yfm offices. "We called all the Yfm staff together and explained the situation to them before Fana went public. It felt as if the whole organisation was behind Yfm and Fana – that together we would win this thing. At that stage, I still thought it would only be a few weeks before Fana on ARVs would be back at work. In fact it was the beginning of a journey that got crazier and crazier.

"The minute his positive status was out in the public arena, dozens of interventions we had never thought of occurred and a host of people we had never heard of came knocking at our and his doors offering solutions. Despite thinking we had a tight understanding with Fana on how to handle these things, it soon became apparent that we had very little control over the situation. I interacted frequently with him initially, and while all I wanted to know was how he was doing on his medication regimen, all he wanted to know was when he could get back on air again despite the fact that he was getting sicker."

On July 21, 2003, Dirk sent the following letter to Fana:

This letter is intended as a written record of the verbal agreement reached between Yfm and yourself when it became clear you were no longer able to perform your duties as presenter in mid-April 2003, and as a formal notice from Yfm to you requiring you to comply with your side of the agreement.

Yfm undertook to:

* Guarantee that your position with the company as both a weekday and Sunday presenter would remain until you were well enough to again perform your duties
* To continue to pay your salary until you were able to return to work or until your existing contract expires
* To pay for your reasonable medical and counselling needs in relation to your HIV virus
* To assist you practically and financially to obtain the best medical and psychological support which is reasonably available
* To assist you to go away to recuperate
* To protect you from the media except where we jointly decided it was in the best interest of yourself, Yfm and/or the HIV/Aids debate to engage with the media

You, Fana Khaba, undertook to:

* Follow the advice of proper medical experts to eat properly, rest, avoid stress and generally to do all in your power to ensure that you understand the nature of the HI virus and what is required of changes in your lifestyle to ensure that you get better as soon as possible
* Consult regularly with proper medical practitioners to assist you and to stick to whatever was agreed between yourself and the medical practitioners
* Co-operate with the agreed upon media strategy
* Produce, as soon as you felt well enough, a daily audio diary that would both keep contact with your listeners and be an educational and inspirational message on HIV/Aids

Yfm believes we have stuck to the letter and spirit of our verbal agreement. We are concerned, however, that you have to date, inter alia:

* Not rested as advised and have involved yourself in a number of new projects which could only have created more stress in your life without any consultation with Yfm
* Have not accounted for how over R10 000 given to you for medical and recuperation purposes over and above your monthly salary has been spent
* Have granted several interviews to the media with no consultation with Yfm
* Have unilaterally gone on air at Yfm with no consultation with operations manager and have constantly interfered with Yfm staff
* Have had several media discussions with other media institutions about working for or with them with no prior consultation with Yfm
* Have generally conducted yourself in a way which can only exacerbate your condition including promising people a host of things which you say Yfm will apparently sort out, without discussing these things with Yfm, and being constantly on the move when you are above all else required to rest.

I found this letter moving. How many South African companies officially advise their HIV-positive employees to take time off to rest and avoid stress? How many promise to keep their sick employees' jobs open and pay their medical and counselling expenses? How many consider the wider interests of society when deciding whether to engage publicly in the HIV/Aids debate? Presumably the humanity displayed here reflected the progressive origins of Yfm and the strong internal culture it had built up on the back of it. Yfm referred to itself as the Yfm family. Externally, this notion of community was played out in its offshoot, Ycares, which organised visits to Aids hospices and orphanages by Yfm DJs – including Khabzela.

I asked Greg why he thought Fana had refused to take the path that would have best guaranteed his health.

He said he thought that the very qualities that had got Fana to where he was: his refusal to accept what was offered to him and his determination to achieve his dreams had made him stubborn and single-minded. "He didn't believe in his limitations. He didn't allow the system to fence him in and that mindset might work for you at a certain stage but if it makes you stubborn, it might work against you later on."

The other, equally persuasive reason, according to Greg, was that while part of Fana was modern and westernised, another part was rooted in African traditional understanding of misfortune. This schism, he believed, split his family as well and they came to play a fatal part in Fana's choices, particularly when dementia began to affect his reasoning. "There was a Christian force and a traditional African force. He believed in both. He believed both had a place in his heart and in his life. And if they worked together, they would help settle his soul. And unfortunately, when he got ill, these forces went to war with each other. Because half of his family was very religious in terms of Christianity, and the other part of the family was extremely grounded in African values, and all of them were being very selfish and not wanting to understand what he was going through and what it was that he really needed.

"Everybody wanted a piece of him. Even on his deathbed, everybody wanted something out of him, which really broke me. And all he really wanted was to get well and get back to his job and to looking after his family. He just wanted to take whatever steps would make him better: whether it was kneeling down and praying or taking anti-retrovirals or going to *inyangas*. Because there were times when he got ill when his mind wasn't right; when he couldn't make decisions for himself and you had the family and all sorts of other people intervening and I think all of those things just made him worse. All these forces fighting each other so that they can take the glory in the end. I think those things were the biggest factor in his death.

"Because with anti-retrovirals, it's a programme. You have to stay on it. You have to be loyal to it. And because there were all these forces fighting in his head and around him, he couldn't stick to that programme. I don't believe he didn't want to take them. I believe that at some point, he got overpowered by a particular belief and he thought all those western medicines were not going to help him. And he tried this and he tried that and the one doesn't work with the other. There was some woman in Boksburg who gave him yellow pills. There were all sorts of people with all sorts of things and it just got too much. It was just unbearable. You could understand why you could go mad."

Dirk said that he regretted that he was not firmer and more interventionist with Fana and the people around him. "I thought that because we were not experts on HIV/Aids, we did not have the right to intervene strongly and we stepped back whenever another so-called expert stepped forward. But for whatever reason – and Fana had a lot to do with this – many of these interventions ended up going nowhere and when he finally succumbed to the virus all that was left was a host of recriminations all around. Expert against so-called expert, traditional against scientific solutions, nutrition against ARVs.

"Since Fana's death, the debate around HIV has got even more polarised. Every one of the actors in the current debate crossed Fana's and our path and all of them struck me as genuine people striving to find an answer. But I cannot understand why we as South Africans can't build a consensus on the best way to deal with it. Good nutrition is essential for building an immune system that can resist HIV and other viruses. In this respect I am fully behind our President and the Minister of Health. But when one's CD4 count falls below 200, anti-retrovirals are the only and last resort.

"Of course, key to this is the ability of the infected person to radically change their lifestyle. Sadly, Fana was not able to do this. He looked for a miracle solution – one that would change his situation overnight. But no such solution exists."

Edwin Cameron wrote in his wonderful memoir, *Witness to Aids*, of his own initial reluctance to start anti-retroviral therapy. Despite the fact that he believed in their efficacy and he badly needed them – his CD4 count was below 200 and he was suffering from pneumocystis carinii pneumonia, oesophagal thrush and extreme fatigue – he put off taking the drugs for far longer than was sensible.

"Why was I so reluctant to start treatment…?" he mused. "One reason was the side effects I knew that I could expect. The drugs are immensely powerful. They have to be. Powerful enough to reach into the abstruse corners of the body's genetic mechanisms, where HIV replicates, to put a stop to its machinations. So powerful that in doing so, they unavoidably affect other body functions – upsetting the digestive system, causing painful nerve abreactions (tingling, numbness) and redistribution of body fat. Rare toxic reactions, some even fatal – when patients or their damaged livers just cannot tolerate the force of the drugs – gave me additional pause.

"But I also feared something starker: that the drugs wouldn't work for me. Dr Johnson told me that his colleagues in rich countries were reporting success rates of about 70%. Wonderful. But this also meant that for almost one third of those starting on treatment in 1997 the drugs did not work. What if I was amongst them?"

Denial, he said, is a common response to Aids. He too experienced it. "Though cognitively accepting that I was infected with HIV, I continued – even as the evidence mounted that I was falling sick – to hope against hope that I would never fall ill with Aids. Despite the unmistakable signals that warned that my immune defences were failing, and that my viral load was rising, I hoped against belief and probability that somehow I would escape."

# № 15

I was puzzled by the Khabas' animosity towards Sibongile, and asked Mrs Khaba why they were so angry with her. She explained it thus: "I used to like her. I wanted Fana to get married to her but the way she treated us and treated Fana … Point number one: I spoke to her before Fana *lobola*ed her and I told her what I would like her to do with the children, which is: accept them as Fana's children. Which she didn't and that hurt Fana because he loved his children. He would have liked that his children come and visit him. She used to grumble that she's cleaned the house, now they are dirtying the house. Why didn't she have children of her own? She was young. I spoke to her father about that: what was wrong with her that she can't have children?"

Mrs Khaba herself paid some of Sibongile's *lobola*. This seemed to exacerbate the annoyance she felt at Sibongile's failure to bear children. "I helped Fana because he wanted to pay *lobola* after buying a new car. R10 000. It was a lot. For the R10 000 that he paid for Sibongile, she brought nothing along with her. She loved Fana's status and the comfort of his home and things that she used to get from him. Fana used to spoil her.

"Sibongile is not a nice person. She did not nurse Fana. I left my home to go and stay with them because we did not want her to carry all that burden. We knew she was young. Me and my two daughters, Tsidi and Rose, the three of us were there. And when Fana woke in the morning, because he didn't sleep long, Sibongile would sleep. We used to wake up, clean the place, do the washing, do the cooking for Fana. He used to like his Jungle Oats in the morning and a cup of tea.

"When we got there, we found piles and piles of dirty washing. Fana's clothes were all dirty. He used to do that himself when he was young. But when he stayed with Sibongile, we thought Sibongile was going to take over."

This condemnation of Sibongile as inadequate housewife and possible source of Fana's misfortune was echoed by Mpho Mhlongo: "Sibongile wasn't a good wife," he said. "There was no fridge in the house. They ate out all the time. The family went to a *sangoma* and they said there's a woman behind this."

Mpho said he had once seen inside Fana's cupboard. "Every sock had a cut in it, so did every jacket lining – in the same place."

Sibongile shuddered when she talked about the Khaba family. "Jesus, they hated me so much, it scared me. I was thinking: 'Where did that come from? What did I do that was so horrible?' I was scared for my own life. Those *inyangas* they go to; they can get some *muti* for me. Because that's what they believe in, so why wouldn't they do that to another person?"

Sibongile said the first indication of tension came early in 2003 when Fana's family wanted her family to hold an *umvuma*.

"This is a traditional ceremony to welcome him into the family. When he paid *lobola* for me, my father hadn't done that. He lost his job just as he was about to do it. So it was basically a financial issue because it's a big party. It was not that they didn't want to hold the ceremony for him.

"My father said: 'Okay, we'll do the ceremony but I would like us to consider the fact that Fana can't walk. Why can't we come together as two families and look at the wellbeing of these two children? Let's look at what we can do to help them build the relationship, to build their trust. The ceremony will be done at some point. When they are ready to be married we will do it.'

"But Fana's family said: 'No, we want it done now.'

"So my family sat together and said: 'if that's what these people want, let's give it to them.' My father went and gave them the dates: we are doing the ceremony on such and such a date. And you know what? They didn't respond to my father's letter. I took it to mean that they wanted to get rid of me. They said I had to come back to my father's house and stay here till they do the ceremony. I said: 'I have to go and see Fana.' So I would go occasionally and see him but I wouldn't sleep over. His sisters and his mother had already occupied the house.

"Then Tsidi started coming up with allegations that I had bewitched him. When I look at it, it means that they thought I was after Fana's things. They thought maybe if anything happened to Fana, I would get his things. So they had to get rid of me before that happened. Why else would they turn against me just when Fana starts getting ill? Before that, we were best friends. And I knew that I had nothing to fight for. There was no money. It was just the appliances in the house and the cars. That's all."

But Sibongile said that part of her had expected problems with the family. "If a man passes away, it's a big issue. People start saying you are responsible for his death. When you pass away, they say, 'ag, it's God's will'. Look at my case. Everything was okay. All of a sudden, Fana starts getting ill and things turned sour. It happens to people who had something while they were living, like, say, they had businesses. The family always feels that they have the rights over whatever it is that he owned or he worked for. They feel that you are nothing. You are not their child; you are not their sister. It has happened in my family. My family has done it to other people. That is why it was maybe easier for me to deal with because it happens every day in our culture.

"In Fana's case, it was even worse because he was ill and everybody knew what was wrong with him. But still they said he was bewitched. You're the bad guy so they have the right to take whatever they want. There's another friend of mine whose husband was shot. I mean how can you bewitch a person who was shot? They said she bought the people to kill him. They took her out of the house; they took everything from the house and she just left with her three kids. It's sad but it happens."

After talking to all of them, I did think that Mrs Khaba's resentment against Sibongile was partly because she thought she had broken a pact. Mrs Khaba thought that Sibongile would rein in her wild son. Mrs Khaba suspected that this didn't happen because of Sibongile's inability to conceive. She was convinced, however unfairly, that some murky event in Sibongile's past was the reason for this. Fana didn't stay at home because Sibongile didn't provide a proper, child-filled home for him. And, to make it worse, Mrs Khaba also felt that she had been cheated out of the grandchildren she longed for.

Tsidi's motives were probably slightly different. She had looked after Fana when he was a child; she had protected him from street bullies. With Mrs Khaba constantly away at work, Tsidi and her sisters – themselves only children – would effectively have been surrogate mothers to their young siblings. When Fana came into money, Tsidi and her children benefited, a luxury they would have grown used to and to which she might have felt she was entitled, given her own role in his upbringing. And she, unlike Fana, still struggled financially as an unemployed single mother. Fana's death deprived her of a newfound comfort zone. One could have imagined her being outraged at the prospect of a newcomer to the family like Sibongile sharing what little there was left of it. Yet, while Sibongile would have had a lot to gain from the relationship while Fana was alive – the status of being a celebrity's wife as well as material benefits such as expensive clothes and a relatively lavish lifestyle – all she was left with when he died was an incurable disease.

By the time I met Sibongile and the Khabas, the relationship between them had already fallen apart and there was a lot of animosity on both sides. What was more difficult to work out was what Sibongile had meant to Fana. In many ways, she would have represented for him the same moral centre as his mother did. She was young and virginal when they met: he plucked her straight from school. She came from a strong religious background and, unlike Fana, still went to church regularly. Although Sibongile herself patronised the Rhema church or a local Sowetan charismatic Christian church, her sister was a Jehovah's Witness so she would have understood where Fana was coming from. She did not drink, smoke or hang out at shebeens or clubs. Her clothes were modest and demure. Yet, even, at her lowest ebb, Sibongile exuded a confident sensuality. I had no doubt that she was able to wield considerable power over susceptible men.

Sibongile was with Fana through the most momentous periods of his life: getting his job at Yfm; moving from Soweto to the suburbs; getting ill. At Yfm, he had been very public about his adoration of her, rhapsodising about her beauty on air. And she was his official partner, despite the many unofficial ones. The nurses at Brenthurst said he had cried out for her at night when he was delirious from fever – although at one point, he seemed to have bought into the theory that she was the one who had bewitched him.

He had made the phone call to Nonosi breaking off their relationship when he *lobola*ed Sibongile, which would seem to imply commitment. But Kenny Ndaba believed that this was instigated by Mrs Khaba, who was becoming increasingly concerned about Fana's womanising and wanted him to settle down with one woman. In fact, it was Kenny's older brothers who had conducted the *lobola* negotiations with the Radebe family on behalf of the Khabas.

Kenny explained the *lobola* ceremony thus: "It is the male's family asking for friendship from the female's family with a view to her being our bride." Initial negotiations, he said, involved the gift of R100 and a bottle of spirits. Beer wouldn't do. It had to be something expensive. Kenny's brothers were called in because you have to be married, to have experience of marriage to be able to conduct *lobola* negotiations with any authority. And, presumably, you should be male.

But Greg Maloka, who saw a lot of Fana in the last few years of his life and was close to him, believed that Sibongile was his emotional anchor. "He was an extremely powerful individual. At some point, the entire culture revolved around his ideas. But he was a powerful individual who needed to be centred; to be loved and taken care of. And I think Sibongile was the one person who kept him centred. She was the one person who knew him wholly. The rest of us knew the macho, big-headed guy who could sort out anything but she would know him when he was at his lowest. She was the person he chose to be with and live with. He had the deepest of love for her.

"Fana was very conservative in many ways. But it was amazing how he had wanted Sibongile to be independent, to work, to empower herself. You would expect him to want somebody who would sit at home: someone to whom he could say: 'Shut up. I'm bringing the bread here so don't mess with me.' His mentality was like that in many ways but when it came to Sibongile, it was different. Of course they had their problems. Like in any relationship, there were ups and downs. Sometimes he'd say: 'That's it. I'm going to kick her out.' The next day, he's tired; he's just going to pick her up from wherever she is and go home and watch DVDs with her. So I'm convinced he loved her dearly.

"Sometimes families become selfish with their own. They start seeing the spouse as a person who is taking the jewel away from us, who is ripping off all the benefits." Greg also saw Sibongile's inability to have children as an exacerbating factor: "I think they viewed that very seriously; that she basically has him to herself. The attention they got from him obviously started to dwindle because the man has his own home to look after. That would cause a rift."

Greg too believed the vilification of Sibongile was related to disputes over material possessions. "I would imagine a scenario where a sister as strong-willed as Tsidi would have wanted all her brother's things to be her decision. He loved his mother dearly. He worshipped the ground she walked on. But I think he was the one person in that entire family that kept it together. The family began to depend on him for inspiration, for motivation, but also for resources. He started not to be able to cope with the immense pressure that was put on him. But, like any other guy, you don't show that. It's always: I can do it. If you need, I can provide. If my mother wants this, I can't say no to my mother. Or if my child needs this, or my girlfriend needs this. And he couldn't say no. He was very giving. And I think largely the family used that. Some people within his family took advantage of that.

"Sibongile had to come out of being Khabzela's wife to being Sibongile, an individual. I think she herself had to battle with the temptation of being a wife to a famous guy. He was doing that as well. He was looking to empower her. I remember him saying to me: 'I really wanna take this girl to school, take her to driving school. I don't want her to sit around and be useless. Sometimes she just annoys me because she doesn't wanna do anything.' But he had the deepest of love for her."

Sibongile said her attraction to Fana was based on the fact that he was so different to herself. "He was a free person. When he wanted to say something, he would say it and he didn't care. I think that was the main attraction: that he was free and he believed in himself so much. But I guess at the time I was still growing myself; learning things about life, about people."

But she was also strongly aware of his shortcomings. "With him, it was always about me, me, me. You can't always say 'me, me, me'. At some point, it has to be other people also. But then I guess we meet people, we get attracted to them and we forget other things that are important, like your backgrounds, your belief, your vision.

"And you imagine yourself in that vision and you ask yourself: do you really want to be in it? And I looked at it and I thought: we had different visions. There is nothing common about me and you. Fine, you are free-spirited but there are other important things. I value other people. I'm not arrogant. I treat people with respect. He was very arrogant.

"And I love reading. I love studying. He doesn't believe in that. He believes you can do it on your own. You could never sit with Fana like this for five minutes and talk. That would be highly impossible. He didn't listen. He talked and talked but he couldn't listen. When he's listening, he's thinking of what he's going to say.

"I looked at all those things and I thought: 'What are you doing here?' But at the time, I wanted to see that he's perfect. He's everything I want."

Sibongile said she was very keen to get a job but that Fana's jealousy was always an issue. "He was very insecure and his jealousy was getting to me because he would feel that he had to buy me things to stay. I mean he would look at me and think: 'Oh, you're so beautiful. What are you doing with me? You could find another man out there. You could just charm him and when you've charmed him, you could go.' But it's not about that. If I didn't love him, I wouldn't be there. So I did feel that he was doing those things for me because he wanted me to stay. And he thought maybe I loved those things more than him, the cars and whatever. But it was not like that. Fana always felt he had to pay people to love him. He had to pay people to be with him. He didn't feel he was worthy to be loved, whether he had money or not. He always felt that, in order for them to be around, he had to show them that he could pay."

When I met Sibongile, I was impressed by her articulateness, her intelligence, her courage in dealing with a situation that might well have felled a lesser woman. I interviewed her several times and watched a slow determination gather in her to find a job, to make her own way in life and not be dependent on a man, as she had been on Fana.

She said she had always dreamed of becoming a flight attendant. I had a strong desire to help Sibongile in any way I could. Not only because she had been dealt such a rough hand but also because she had been so generous in helping me with my research. Cheryl Carolus was then CEO of South African Tourism and I knew that she was strongly supportive of women afflicted by HIV so I asked if she could help. Sibongile had told me she had done a course in IT at Damelin College and, as luck would have it, there was at the time a vacancy for a data processor at South African Tourism. Cheryl arranged for Sibongile to be interviewed for the job. The interview itself went well. Sibongile's personability and obvious intelligence shone through. But, unfortunately, the written test didn't go as well.

I typed up Sibongile's CV and emailed it off whenever I saw a job she might qualify for. But we had little luck until she phoned me one day to say she had an interview for a marketing position. She was very excited when she made it to the second interview and then I got a miserable, frantic call. The company was insisting on seeing her certificate from Damelin but the latter were refusing to give it to her because she still owed them R7 000. It turned out that Fana, the ever-jealous boyfriend, had accused her of having an affair with her lecturer and so had refused to pay the fees.

I had begun by then to feel slightly dismayed by the responsibility I appeared to have taken on. Every couple of weeks, there'd be a missed call from Sibongile on my cell phone. I'd call her back but neither of us would have much to report. Then, early in 2005, she called to say she had an apprenticeship at a travel agency. She was clearly elated and so was I. Then she said matter of factly that she needed a world atlas, a calculator and a punch. From me, that is. I felt like a parent with a demanding schoolchild but dutifully went off to CNA to buy them.

We arranged to meet at the Carlton Centre. She looked every inch the young professional in a tailored black dress that emphasised her neat figure. She was glowing with confidence and happiness. Men cast admiring glances at her and she preened in response. I handed over her goodies with a smile and prayed her good fortune would last.

# № 16

"The woman in Boksburg" mentioned by Greg seemed, for some inexplicable reason to have made more of an impression on Fana than any other individual healer. Also referred to as "Dr Irene" and, in fact from Brakpan, another nondescript East Rand suburb, she appeared to have acquired mythical status in Fana's mind and he raved about her to anyone who would listen.

The late Kumza, for instance: "He always believed in Irene's medicines. He believed in herbs. He said: 'herbs are better than anti-retrovirals because those ones can kill me'. He told me: 'don't let them make me drink them'. I'll tell you one thing about Irene's Amazing Grace. Khabzela couldn't walk. But after he drank her pills, he started walking. He came back. He was, like, getting fat, and getting his weight back."

And Dirk: "He thought she was his salvation. He thought he was going to be cured. It was almost like an angel had come to him. He said when he arrived at her house, she was sitting in a rocking chair on the *stoep* and she got up and she said to him in Afrikaans: 'Khabzela, I've been waiting for you all my life.' God had told her he was sending his special angel to her. And then they prayed together and she gave him Amazing Grace. At that stage, he couldn't walk at all. After that, like literally the next day, he was able to walk. By walk, I mean hobble extremely slowly and painfully for a while. And he believed that he didn't need anti-retrovirals or anything else. That he was well on his way to being cured. She told him that by August, he would be cured."

In late July, when I met Fana for lunch at Cresta mall, he was still taking Amazing Grace, still believing it would cure him, although by then his own physical deterioration must have let in a little doubt.

Masi Makhalemele also had a vivid memory of the impression left by Irene: "Irene was the first port of call and she emphasised over and over again that he mustn't take ARVs. He said Irene said they would make him sick; 'They will kill me.' He kept on saying he mustn't take ARVs till he had finished her treatment. I think he listened to her because she was white."

Sibongile beamed when she talked about Irene. Her intervention marked a brief hopeful hiatus in a dreadful period. It was on the morning of May 21, she said, some five weeks after Fana had discovered his status. "Fana's family had been to some *inyanga* and got him some medicine that he was supposed to drink. They were about to give him the medicine when there is a knock at the door. It's this woman. She heard about Fana's story on the radio and she said: 'I have to help him.' She didn't know where Fana stayed but she knew he stayed in Emdeni and everyone in Emdeni knows where Khabzela stays. She went there and asked people 'where does Khabzela stay' and a young boy said 'come I'll show you.' When she gets [to his mother's house] there, she finds Fana's niece and she said: 'Please take me to Fana's place.' So, in the morning, Fana's niece comes with the woman. The woman said: 'I didn't sleep. I was looking for you all over. I don't know if it was God but somehow I had to find you.' And then she says: 'I'm taking you to Irene right now.'"

The woman explained that both she and her husband were HIV positive. The husband had been terminally ill in

Johannesburg Hospital and Irene had saved him. "The woman said Irene is a Christian. Whatever she does it comes from God. So they both went to Irene and the husband started taking Irene's herbs. And then the husband got better because he was not mixing it with anything. Irene told them: 'Look, you need to do this, you need to do that,' and the husband did exactly what Irene told him. And he got better. The husband three months later went back to the hospital where he was taking treatment because with Irene's herbs, it doesn't cause any conflict. You can take the ARVs and take her herbs at the same time. They are both medicine. And the doctors were shocked because he went there walking and he was okay. And they wanted to know what he did because it's a miracle. And the husband said no because at that time Irene didn't want people to know about her. I guess it was still a pilot thing."

Listening to Sibongile, some things became apparent. It did not occur to her that it was the ARVs, rather than Irene's pills, that had caused the man's miraculous recovery. For some reason, she and the couple had been far more impressed by Irene. But it also struck me that Irene was equated in their minds with 'medicine'; white western medicine. She was not jealous and territorial; she allowed ARVs as well. But she also brought in divine agency and emotion, which western medical practitioners failed to do – probably quite short-sightedly, if you look at where most of their Aids patients were coming from. And she was, as Masi pointed out, white. Possibly, Irene presented the point of reconciliation Fana so desperately needed between his warring Christian and traditional African beliefs.

The way Sibongile presented it there was a very immediate and dramatic choice between the traditional

African way – the *inyanga's* medicine about to be poured down Fana's throat – and the woman at the door promising a white, Christian miracle. "Somehow, God just brings this to me: Fana is not going to drink that medicine. He must not drink it. Let's take him to Irene now.... And the woman said: 'I'm going to put him in my car and take him to Irene.'"

Dirk said he asked Fana later: "How could you just get in a car with a perfect stranger? I mean, you're as sick as anything. And he said: 'I was going to be cured'."

Between them, Sibongile and the woman carried Khabzela into her waiting car. There followed a long journey, first to fetch the woman's husband and then, finally, to Brakpan.

"Some of the things that happened, I can't explain," said Sibongile. "That's why I feel Irene was sent by God somehow. When we got there, Irene was waiting for us. She said she had been praying to God: 'Bring this person to me. I know I can help him but if you want me to help him, just bring him here.'

"Irene had read about Fana in the *Sowetan*. She called the *Sowetan*, wanting Fana's number. The *Sowetan* said they couldn't give out private numbers. And the next morning, Fana was at her doorstep. It was like a divine connection.

"When we got in there, she said: 'Let's pray.' We prayed. We prayed. She said: 'I'm going to help you. You're going to be fine. There are people who come in here who are even worse than you and they leave here walking. But you cannot do it if you do not believe.'

"*Ag*, Fana was so excited. Irene gave him the three pills. He drank them and we went home. That night, he drank the pills again because Irene said he should. He was totally paralysed then. He couldn't walk. Irene said to him: 'I'm giving you ten

**180**

days and you will be on your feet'. You know, it was hardly twenty-four hours and he could walk.

"The following morning, I opened my eyes and Fana was not there in the bed beside me. I thought 'Oh my god, he's fallen down somewhere' and I ran into the kitchen and he was standing there, making tea. He said: 'Sweetie, I can walk.' I nearly fainted. I thought: 'Maybe I'm dreaming.' I said: 'It's a miracle.' You know it's a miracle.

"That's when Fana started to believe in Irene. He wanted nothing but Irene. I thought the mistake was he believed in Irene more than in the pills, more than himself and God. He didn't want to hear anything about anti-retrovirals. He didn't want to hear the words 'anti-retrovirals'. Sis Angie [Diale] was saying to him: 'Look, drink the herbs but also drink the anti-retrovirals because anti-retrovirals are made specifically to deal with the virus within you, to fight the virus. The herbs are good to boost your immune system.' He took [the anti-retrovirals] for a week. He said he was getting worse. It was in his mind that they are going to kill him. So they couldn't do much in his body because he didn't believe in them. After a week, he said: 'No more anti-retrovirals. Say anti-retrovirals and I'm going to scream.' He never took them again. They were just lying there in the house."

A couple of weeks after Fana's death, Sibongile managed to find a number for 'Dr Irene' as she called her and, with some trepidation, I dialled it. When a woman answered: "Hello, East Rand Paving," I assumed I had the wrong number. But no, it turned out that I was indeed talking to Irene. I explained what I was doing and asked if I could come and see her. Given that Fana had now died, I expected a hostile, defensive response. But, on the contrary, she said she would be very happy to see me and we settled on a date a couple of days away.

There was a mighty storm the day I went to see Irene. Thunder boomed, lightening flashed against the sky and rain and hail battered my car. I wondered if it was God wanting to make another statement. He or she seemed so far to have been very vocal in matters relating to Irene.

The combination of driving rain and my non-existent sense of direction necessitated several phone calls to Irene for me to find her house, but she was endlessly sweet and patient. Brakpan, it is safe to say, is pretty hideous. It started off as a dormitory for white mine workers, most of whom were racist, conservative and without any discernable taste. It is still ugly, drab and suburban – lots of low-slung, face-brick housing, narrow streets and, it seems, a furniture shop offering long-term finance at exorbitant rates on every corner. With the election coming up, every pole was festooned with political posters, some for the New National Party (NNP) and some for the ANC. Years ago it would have been the National Party (NP), and the Herstigte Nationale Party (HNP), South Africa'a most extreme right wing party. But Brakpan, like most other low cost towns, has quickly become far more racially mixed than the more expensive northern suburbs. Part of the reason for my disorientation was that I had expected something grander of this alleged angel of mercy – or at least more tasteful.

When I finally found Irene's home, I saw dimly through a sheet of rain and hail the connection with East Rand Paving: a large sign advertising it was stuck to the front of an ugly, double-storey face-brick building. I looked in vain for a rocking chair – or, indeed for a verandah. They must have been figments of Fana's disease-addled imagination.

I ran to the front door and Irene answered it immediately. She too, was a surprise: a little daffy granny, quintessentially suburban in her neatly coiffuired, dyed auburn hair and rayon leopard-print shirt. I was ushered through an entrance hall crowded with large, crude statues of elephant and buffalo to her office, a small, rectangular room to the left of the entrance hall, lined with filing cabinets and, at the far wall, a desk on which several telephones sat. All seemed to be ringing at once. Irene rushed to answer one: "East Rand Paving," she said. And arranged for her son to go round to a local house to give a quote for paving a driveway. After she had put the phone down and made a note of the call, she explained that, in between saving lives, she helped her sons with their paving business. The very bizarreness of this combination rather endeared her to me. She was entirely without any air of self-importance, despite the preposterous claims delivered in her soft, quick voice.

"We've seen them come from death unto life," she said. And then she read me her mission statement: "In 1998, HIV/Aids was the topic of discussion and concern. People were dying at such a tempo that a cure was on everyone's lips. I do believe the Holy Spirit dawned on me. A force greater than myself led me to believe this was a divine intervention and the only cure as the Holy Spirit is like a consuming fire. Despite the negativity, mocking and criticism, I had not been disappointed. My highest expectations were met and my first patient with full-blown Aids recovered and tested negative after using the medicine for only four months. Realising that this is a God-given miracle, I decided to call it Amazing Grace. My mission is to reach out to the oppressed and dying. The Lord confirmed through prophecy that he had given in front of me an open door no man shall close. I would like to cater for countries such as Uganda, Malawi, Nairobi and the rest of Africa."

Irene, sixty-two, did not have much formal education. Born and brought up in Brakpan, she left school with only a standard eight qualification. She got married at the age of twenty-one to a South African of Greek extraction. "My husband was very handsome," she said proudly, "I'll just show you my wedding album. Do you want to see it?"

She and her husband had four children and all was going well when tragedy struck for the first time. Her eldest son, Georgie, was staying with Irene's mother near Nelspruit when he ate poisonous berries. "He started complaining about severe pain in the stomach. We took him to Nelspruit to the doctor and he said we better take him straight away to Joburg. They admitted him there and over the phone – I'll never forget this – the doctor said: 'Your child has developed brain cancer. We give him three months to live.'

Irene was convinced it was the poison from the berries that had caused the cancer. "Definitely! Definitely!" she said. "The poison is a very deadly poison. There was nothing wrong with him before he went there. It was only after he ate the stuff [that he got ill]."

The death of her son on May 1, 1970, she said, propelled her into the business of saving lives. Until then, she seemed to have been a fairly normal person, a devoted mum of four with a nice Greek husband who ran a takeaway business from a building adjacent to the house.

First, she was jolted out of the faith she had been brought up in – the Dutch Reformed Church. During this traumatic period, the local DRC minister rebuffed her because she had married a Greek Orthodox man and "you know a Greek, they don't close their shops to go to church, that's for sure."

At her child's bedside, she met a pastor from the Full Gospel Church who was so different from the judgemental, territorial DRC minister that she was swept off her feet.

She launched into evangelical-speak. "The moment he walked in, there was such a radiance on his face, it felt as if the angels came in with him. And when he prayed for my child, the anointing of the Lord was so upon him that the tears ran over his cheeks. And it was so awesome. It made such an impression on my life. And then I was born again.

"After my child died, I was devastated. He looked so thin and worn out but his face was so radiant. I laid him out on the bed and I spoke to the Lord: I said: 'Please father, just put your hand on him so the spirit of infirmity can go from him.' But when I looked into his face, he was gone. My child didn't come alive. And I said 'But why, Lord?' I felt betrayed. Then my mother phoned the pastor and when he came, he spoke so nicely, he said: 'The Lord took this child while he was pure in heart and pure in mind'."

While she was talking to me, Irene was sobbing, the pain apparently as fresh as at the time of her son's death more than three decades before. She felt now that there was a divine purpose for her loss. "I could not understand how the Lord could allow this child to be taken. It was only much later when I got involved with people with Aids that I could understand. Because I could not feel their pain, I couldn't feel compassion for them if I hadn't been there. That made a very big difference in my life."

Irene had made such a dramatic impression on Fana, yet his impression on her was much more hazy.

"Did he tell you his story? Why did he stop coming? The

very first day, the brother and him came. Somebody else brought them. One of my previous patients. I said: 'Do you mind if we pray for him?'

"The brother spoke on his behalf. He said: 'No. He doesn't need prayer.'

"I looked him in the face. I said: 'Do you need a miracle?'

"He said: 'Yes.'

"I said: 'Let's speak to the Lord about that.'

"And I led him to the Lord. Because the person has to ask the Lord to come into your heart and into your life, to forgive you all the sins. He can't take your sins away. And I said: 'Lord, come into my heart, forgive me all my sins, wash me whiter than snow, write my name in your book of life and say I surrender to you, Lord, my body, soul and spirit. I shall not die, but live.'"

It was immediately clear to her, said Irene, that Fana was suffering from Aids. "When you go through his symptoms, then straightaway you can see the condition. He was so powerless, unable to stand by himself."

She showed me Khabzela's record sheet which noted that he came on May 21 and then again on June 28. His symptoms were given as severe headaches; fatigue, darker completion (sic), bedridden, and hot and painfull feet (sic). The diagnosis was pwa (person with Aids).

She said she knew what the symptoms of Aids were. "Night sweats, severe headaches, oral and vaginal thrush, the drop. You know, sexual-related diseases. The brain normally goes and they get very brain disorientated. They're extremely tired. Most have got shingles. They've got swollen glands, they've palpitations through stress. They've got very brown lines on their nails, their complexion becomes very dark, they've got this itching and scratching. Many times they are already busy dying from the tuberculosis. They're normally bedridden and then the other symptom is shoulder blade pain; lower back pain and painful feet. Those are the main symptoms you can look for."

There was something about Irene that was so naïve and defenceless that one wanted to protect her from herself. The daffy little granny was more than image, I thought. She was homey and confiding; hauling out photo albums to show me pictures of her handsome husband, her dead son, Georgie, her three surviving children and two grandchildren. And the constant, very pedestrian interruptions to her religious ravings as she answered the phone to take orders for either East Rand Paving or Amazing Grace.

I had explained I was a journalist. These were early days and I was not yet sure where my research would end up. At the time it might have been a long article in Y Mag, which was what I told her. Yet she kept showing me confidential information about her patients, lab results showing viral loads and CD4 counts. She gave me Fana's records – the copying machine wasn't working. And then implored me not to make any claims on her behalf because the Medicines Control Council could close her down if I did. Although the real enemy in her eyes seemed to be the pharmaceutical companies: "They are the people who are going to give me a hard time."

Afterwards I struggled with this dilemma. It seemed to me that she was one of many people giving false hope to desperate people – and making money out of it. One of the vultures around the Aids epidemic, a group to which, as I have pointed out before, I belong. I too am profiting from this epidemic. If

Fana had not died, I would not have a story. But I am not selling vitamin pills to people and telling them it will make them rise from the dead. I thought that Irene was benign in intent, though. I genuinely believed that she thought she was doing good. "It was never my intention to get rich out of dying people," she said. "My main aim is to restore dignity."

The compromise I reached with myself was that I would not repeat the claims Irene made to me but she had also made these claims to Fana, who had broadcast them to everyone who would listen. Although I must add here that, as far as I could make out, the injunctions against ARVs were all Fana's. Irene never at any point told me that ARVs were poisonous. Indeed she had no problem with their being taken in conjunction with her Amazing Grace, although she would maintain that they were unnecessary. What she did say was: "Look, it's not my field. But many people are complaining that they exhaust their medical aids, you see. And it's a well known fact that many people died from the side effects. Amazing Grace does combat a lot of the side effects."

Irene wouldn't tell me what was in her Amazing Grace tablets, but said the ingredients "you can find on the shelves at Pick 'n Pay." It was the invisible divine ingredient that she believed gave them their potency. "That's why I call it Amazing Grace," she said. "The honour and the glory goes to the Lord. I take no credit for myself."

Patients were advised to take two pills three times a day. Consultation was free, but the pills cost R100 a month with an extra R40 if they wanted them delivered by courier which, apparently, many patients did.

About two thousand people were using Amazing Grace, she said. 90% of her patients were black. Most were HIV positive.

The building next door, which used to be her husband's takeaway, had been turned into her consulting rooms. For years, Irene helped her Greek husband sell fish and chips from this same room. Then, eight years before, there was an armed robbery at the takeaway and her husband was shot. "He had such suffering. It was terrible seeing him die slowly. He lost all the will to live. When he realised he'd never walk again, he had no will to live any longer." In fact, he lived for another seven years, only dying in July 2003.

Their livelihood gone, Irene began selling her potions from the old takeaway while her sons started the paving business. But Irene felt that it was too dangerous for her to work in the consulting rooms herself. Criminals might come in, pretending to be patients. So Irene herself no longer conducted consultations. They were conducted by her assistants. Pastors did the praying bit. "They call me if it's really an emergency or they are insisting to see me." She employed six people. "I've got a qualified Aids counsellor; two of the ladies are working with the files and the others are doing the filling in of new patients."

There was no attempt at physical examination. Patients' symptoms were ticked off a list and a diagnosis made. Treatment didn't vary, whatever the symptoms. Everyone got Amazing Grace, dispensed with a prayer. There seemed to be several pastors wandering in and out – all black and from various evangelical churches. The consulting room itself was a drab affair, done up in dull browns. There were three or four people draped limply over chairs. It was not a cheery place.

Irene came up with her recipe for Amazing Grace in typical homespun way. "I grew up with remedies. You know, like lemons and stuff. And then there was this particular formula that I mixed and I gave it to people with skin conditions." This had miraculous results, she said. And then, one day, a black man walked into the takeaway and while ordering his fish and chips, she noticed a shocking pink spot on his nose. "I said: 'Sorry, can I ask you something personal?'

"He said: 'Yes, madam.'

"I whispered: 'You don't by any chance have HIV?'

"He left in such a hurry. But later he came back and he called me to one side and he said: 'My wife died in 1992 of full-blown Aids.'"

I can't continue with this story because it involves claims Irene doesn't want to make publicly but, essentially, it explains how the homespun remedy for skin conditions evolved into something much more ambitious. I left Brakpan bemused by the effect that this, to me, utterly unimpressive little woman had on Fana.

Masi said she thought it was because Irene was white. I wondered whether it didn't have deeper roots: in Fana's Jehovah's Witness–dominated childhood. All this fundamentalist Christian talk of sins and miracles would have had strong resonance for him. When I met him in July, there were echoes of this. He talked a lot about his sins and how he could redeem himself in God's eyes. It is possible that as his independence and powers of reasoning were being eroded by the virus, as he felt his life ebbing away, these earlier associations with the powerless, infantile state coupled with their promises of a better world beyond the present one might have reasserted their appeal.

# № 17

Within a few weeks, Irene's magic had begun to wear off and Fana was searching for another miracle cure. *Sangoma* Nene, a Swazi who practised in Soweto, had finally rid Satch of the *isidliso* that was killing him after other *sangoma*s had tried and failed despite considerable financial investment on Satch's part. So Satch was very confident that Mr Nene could help his friend, if anyone could. Fana visited *Sangoma* Nene in June and November of 2003. Again, hope flared briefly, only to collapse again into despair.

I asked Satch if he could arrange for me to see *Sangoma* Nene and, after a few phone calls back and forth, we established a time and date. It was a hot summer's day when we pulled up outside *Sangoma* Nene's Jabulani home. It took me longer than usual to shut the drooping passenger door on Satch's *skoroskoro*. I was nervous about this interview. I felt like a confidence trickster. I would go in there, as usual, smiling, charming and unthreatening as possible and then proceed to attempt to breach this man's code of ethics by getting confidential information about a patient without the consent of the family. I didn't know what code of ethics traditional healers operated by, but a conventionally trained doctor would not have been allowed to divulge any such information.

There was no way I could ask the family's permission as they denied he had ever been to *sangoma*s. But I could not shirk this interview. Fana had believed in traditional healers and visited them frequently, as did thousands of other South Africans with

HIV. And, in the end, it was up to *Sangoma* Nene himself to decide whether or not to give me personal information.

The exterior of *Sangoma* Nene's premises was unprepossessing. It was a squat building painted a muddy brown. The side facing the road was boarded up. Peeling black steel sheets had been nailed over broken windows panes.

Satch led me to a gate at the side and we walked down a narrow path to a small back yard which was crammed with six cages. Each held a skinny, yapping dog. "He uses them for hunting," explained Satch. There were two rooms leading off a verandah and, at the far end, a door which led into what had been a garage. The bright light outside was abruptly extinguished. It was a long, gloomy, almost windowless room with benches down each side and, at the road end, an ancient-looking blue van.

This garage appeared to double as the waiting room and there were three women sitting on the benches, one of mixed race. In one corner was a bunch of branches, a couple of drums and some ordinary Christian bibles: an eclectic spiritual mix by the look of it. A blue flag hung from the ceiling.

*Sangoma* Nene came in and my anxieties melted away. He was a delight; a jolly, well-rounded man dressed in a leopard-skin housecoat affair. His feet were bare and his face lit up with a huge smile. "Call me Mr Magic," he exclaimed. I love this, a *sangoma* with a sense of humour.

The women were summarily asked to leave and I sat down on the bench they had vacated. Mr Magic and Satch sat side by side on the bench opposite: two, plump, middle-aged men, prone to periodic fits of chuckles, frequently at my expense. Mr Magic appeared to find my fumbling questions hilarious.

192

His English seemed to be quite good but nevertheless, he spoke mostly in Zulu, with Satch translating. It was almost a double act. Satch seemed to see himself as Mr Magic's agent. First they impressed upon me what a powerful *sangoma* he was. "This coloured lady who was here, she ran all over – to *sangoma*s, doctors, gynaecologists. They told her she'd never get pregnant but she was fortunate enough to be told to come here and today she is very much pregnant." Satch nudged Mr Magic and said: "Even you, Liz, we can make things happen." Both exploded in great belly laughs. Satch was horrified that I didn't have children and was forever proposing his services in remedying this shortcoming of mine.

Then I asked about Fana and suddenly it all got serious. Fana had first visited in June, said Mr Magic. "When he first came here, he had difficulty with his movement and HIV had damaged his kidneys. They were dead. The minute he started coming here for treatment, he started walking. He then thought he was fine. He thought: 'I won't come any more.' And then he started to be sick again. When he came the second time [in November], it was worse. He couldn't move at all. Then he went to hospital for treatment."

Mr Magic explained that he got his healing powers from God. The conduit between God and Mr Magic were the ancestors, who relayed God's instructions concerning what was ailing the patient and how he or she could be cured. In Fana's case, the prescription was water taken from a certain spot in a certain river and subsequently blessed. Fana was too weak to take Mr Magic's usual treatment, traditional herbs. "Fana's tummy was always running. That is why I couldn't give him strong herbs."

It was Mr Magic's herbs that cured Satch. "I travelled many miles visiting *sangoma*s, pastors, prophets, doctors, when I had this problem in my stomach," said Satch, "but they couldn't find what was wrong. Then I saw this old man. He was using African herbs and he saw this snake."

"The *isidliso*?" I asked.

Mr Magic packed up laughing. Satch explained that it was because a white person had come up with this term. This was not something Mr Magic heard every day. But, yes, it was an *isidliso*. However, this was not what Fana had. Fana had what they called *lwazi*.

"What happened," explained Satch, "is that there was a certain lady who played as if she liked Fana and he got hooked and she gave it to him. That is where he contracted this poison."

"Through sex?" I asked.

"No", said Satch. "Somebody can give it to you without having it. They can buy it and bring it to a place where you pass every day and they call your name. It is like a speed trap. You can't see it but it can catch you. And even if thousands of people pass that place where it is, because your name was called it will catch you and go into your body. You can only feel it after two or three months but then it's gone into your body. But he can help you out of it," said Satch, nodding at Mr Magic, who had frequently interjected and corrected this narrative. Outside, the dogs barked.

"Do you believe you can cure HIV?" I asked.

"If you bring a person with HIV when he is very sick, he has a fifty/fifty chance," said Mr Magic via Satch. "The doctors haven't found a cure for this. The anti-retrovirals can only hold the illness. They can't cure you. But on the traditional side, there is nothing that can't be cured. We get rid of the illness by getting rid of the poison. But you must bring the person in the early stages."

I looked at the bibles and asked: "Is this a church?"

"Is this a church?" repeated Satch in Zulu, and Mr Magic packed up laughing again.

"You know it's a church!" he said to Satch.

"Yes, but I'm translating," said Satch huffily.

Anyway, it turned out that Mr Magic doubled as a pastor in a Christian evangelical church called the Apostolic Church in Zion. He held services in this very garage every Sunday and people flocked to them. The garage was too small to hold them and they spilled out into the road.

"People who have companies and come from the suburbs come here to pray," said Satch. "They come here and collect him to take him to their companies and to their houses to get rid of the evil spirits."

And here followed something of a theological discussion. I was curious as to how Mr Magic incorporated his traditional African religious beliefs with Christianity. I explained that the rules in the faith in which I grew up – the Catholic Church – were very strict. There was God, who signified goodness on the one side, and Satan, as evil incarnate on the other. In between were various intermediaries between man and God such as Jesus, Mary and the saints.

His beliefs weren't that different, he said. The ancestors were the intermediaries with God and it was through pastors like him that they communicated with ordinary humans. And he believed in Satan as the evil force. "It's only Satan that can give you those evil powers to come into your body."

As I got up to leave, Satch, ever the hustler, exhorted me to consult Mr Magic. "He will tell you whatever is wrong with you. If you want to own a shopping complex, he will give you the powers to get it. You just need to come for a week."

Mr Magic, who had been nodding and chuckling away at this, said: "Maybe a week is too much. A few days."

"Owning a shopping complex is not high on my list of ambitions, but I'll think about it," I said. And, indeed, as I emerged from that gloomy, evocative place, past the caged, yapping hunting dogs, I thought: well, maybe. Sometime.

Nowadays I live my life according to secular principles but I do believe there is a realm beyond the tangible. Traditional African forms of spirituality have survived successive waves of assault by rival religions. They have proved remarkably strong and resilient. And I can see why. They are highly adaptable, mixing and matching as they go but nevertheless deeply rooted in Africa, its cultures and the natural environment. They seem far more appealing to me than the frozen certainties handed down by the old men in faraway Rome. If there is indeed magic out there, and I ever feel the need to access it, Mr Magic might indeed be my best bet.

# № 18

'Africa's Solution' is, like 'Amazing Grace', a big name, implicit with big promises. Tine van der Maas dosed Fana with Africa's Solution and it was fed to him in a drip along with anti-retroviral drugs at the Brenthurst Clinic. When she was nursing Fana, Tine held telephone consultations with the creator of Africa's Solution, a man whom she referred to with some awe as Professor Barnard.

She gave me Professor Barnard's phone number and I called him up and we arranged to meet on one of his imminent trips to Johannesburg. Professor Barnard turned out to be a biochemist with a PhD whose given name was Hendrik Christoffel Barnard but he went by the name of Dr Chris Barnard, a name redolent of medical miracles. We met at the modest traveller's hotel in Sandton where Dr Barnard was staying for the weekend.

He was an affable, slightly jowly sixty-year-old with light blue eyes and well-cut gray hair. His English was halting and delivered in a strong Afrikaans accent. Dr Barnard had taught in the chemical pathology department at the University of Bloemfontein for twenty years. He left the university in 1998 and, in 2001, started a company called Bermins which manufactured Africa's Solution and other immune-boosting preparations called variously 'Imu-tain', 'Imu-wize' and 'Imu-wize forte'.

To his credit, Dr Barnard was mildly embarrassed by the grandiosity of his product's name. His original intention, he said, was to signify the scientific form of the preparation, which was liquid, as opposed to solid tablet form.

"I started Africa's Solution for the indigenous peoples of this country," he said. "When I left the university, I saw there is no good vitamin preparation on the market for the lower-income group. So I talked to a lot of natural healers. I even talked to a *sangoma* on the Cape Flats, but we did not talk the same language. We looked at a lot of plants used by the people for many years. The whole purpose of the exercise was finding something that [would] attract them to buy vitamins. So we decided on the so-called African potato or Hypoxis."

Dr Barnard gave me sheafs of information on Bermins products. These stated their guiding philosophy as the following: "The molecular function of the body must be sustained at an optimal functional level so that the body can fight disease and cure itself. Bermins products are not medicines, but contain the necessary essential elements of the different systems in the body and in cases of disease, natural products from nature to help the body's fight against the disease in the most natural way possible."

And, under "more details on the ingredients in Bermins products": "Hypoxis (African Potato) Extract: Clinical trials have indicated that roöperol (the biochemical active substance in the African potato extract) has anti-cancer, anti-HIV and anti-inflammatory properties. The anti-HIV and anti-inflammatory properties of roöperol in the extract of the African Potato in Africa's Solution is of great benefit. It brings about a feeling of well-being and slows down the progression of the disease in the HIV-positive person. The traditional use of extracts of the African Potato may further support the HIV-positive person in maintaining his/her weight, strength and a feeling of well being for a much longer period of time."

Included is a list of the ingredients of Africa's Solution. Hypoxis – an extract from African Potato – is by far the dominant one. Every 15ml contains: 500mg of hypoxis; 4mg of grapefruit seed extract; 28mg of sitosterol and sitosterolin; 1mg of B carotene; 12,5mg of Vitamin E; 7.5mg of Vitamin B6; 3.75mg of Vitamin B1; 10mg of Vitamin B2; 3mg of Vitamin B12; 5mg of nicotinamide; 50mg of ascorbic acid; 325mg of folic acid; 52mg of natural anti-oxidant; 50mg of ferro-sulphate and 35mg of olive green leaf extract.

This last ingredient was added to Africa's Solution in 2003 as a result of experiments conducted by Tine van der Maas.

Bermins' newsletter of January 2003 enthused: "Since Africa's Solution has come on the market, we received wonderful and unbelievable stories of people's health improving. What was most interesting was the feedback from Health Educational Services [Tine van der Maas's outfit] who uses Africa's Solution with lemon and olive oil. This cure has been successfully utilised, especially in patients with HIV. Bermins therefore decided to make an improved Africa's Solution containing olive oil. It is now ready to go on the market."

Later, it elaborated: 'This product [Africa's Solution with added olive leaf extract] was used in an independent research project at the Technical University of the Free State on severely ill people. The abnormal biochemistry and haematology of these very ill patients was rectified within a month. The viral load decreased significantly in people with HIV infection. The CD4 counts did not decrease further. It was also used in an extensive program for severe HIV/Aids patients in hospitals in South Africa with miraculous improvements in 90% of all patients (results available from Tine van der Maas).'

In a pamphlet on Africa's Solution, HIV/Aids sufferers were told to take Africa's Solution for life, as well as to 'take one whole lemon, wash well and grate as finely as possible. Put the grated lemon in a big cup and add one tablespoon extra virgin olive oil and one cup of water. When people are very sick, they should use 2 tablespoons Africa's Solution Forte three times per day. If possible, they should also use one or two Imu-Wize tablets per day.' The pamphlet added the rider: 'These food supplements do not replace any medication prescription by a doctor'.

Unlike Tine van der Maas, Dr Barnard did not dispute the value of anti-retroviral drugs. "Since the late nineties, we know the treatment of anti-retroviral drugs causes the viral load to come down," he said. "You need the anti-retroviral drugs in the initial stage to get the body in charge of the virus. The problem is nobody I know of [will use] the drug day by day for twenty or seven or five or three years. They won't use it. And then you get resistance to the drug and you must change the drug and we all know that any virus can mutate. So it is a solution but not the solution. If you repair the body, if you get the biochemical reactions of the body functioning properly, you wouldn't need anti-retrovirals for a long time. Africa's Solution is developed in a scientific way to do just that: to repair the body."

Dr Barnard presented himself as a philanthropist. "I started Bermins and I put all my money into it. I started it mainly to help the government and help the people. I am the executive trustee. There are other trustees but they are trustees in name only. All the ideas at Bermins started with me and end with me. Bermins is me."

And Bermins was doing very well for Dr Barnard. Even though it was only three years old, turnover was already R5 million a year and growing at the phenomenal rate of 25% a month. Dr Barnard said he expected turnover to increase to R5 million a month by the end of 2005. Many major corporations were buying his product for their workers.

It seemed to me that there must be some connection between the healthy growth of Bermins and the very public support given by the Minister of Health, Manto Tshabalala-Msimang, to Tine van der Maas and her homespun Aids remedies. Tine van der Maas was, in turn, a tireless promoter of Africa's Solution. Dr Barnard explained the link. The health minister had been due to give a talk in Cape Town, he said. Tine made two dolls, with a bottle of Africa's Solution in the stomach of each. One was for the minister and one was for the president. Tine accosted Dr Tshabalala-Msimang and presented her with the dolls. A couple of days later, the two had a meeting. This seemed to have been the origin of the Health Minister's infatuation with the lemon juice, olive oil and African potato diet. The minister herself also regularly promoted Africa's Solution. Both Angie Diale and Masi Makhalemele told me that the minister had recommended to them that they take Africa's Solution. Which they dutifully did.

# № 19

Tine called me up early in March 2005 and invited me to a presentation of her latest research. It was all slightly cloak and dagger. I had to phone someone else called Winston to find out where and when the presentation was. Their fear, apparently, was that the presentation would be ambushed by the TAC, the Treatment Action Campaign.

At 6.30pm the following Tuesday, I turned up at the designated spot in Florida, western Johannesburg, to find a motley bunch of dissidents, traditional healers and the white trade unionists whose offices had been lent for the occasion. Winston turned out to be a pleasant Afrikaans man who was also a salesman for Africa's Solution. Tine and her sixty-nine-year-old mother, Nelly, greeted us with a mixture of excitement and nervousness. Half an hour later than scheduled, a screen was erected in a corner of the room and a film began to roll.

The setting was beautiful. Undulating green hills framed a large body of water, the Inanda dam in KwaZulu-Natal, but the subject matter was harrowing. Suppurating ulcers and emaciated limbs were summarily bared and exposed to the close-up gaze of the camera. The illnesses that had given rise to this suffering ranged from Aids and all its associated opportunistic diseases to diabetes, arthritis, cataracts and epilepsy. All, we were told, had been successfully treated with olive oil, garlic, lemon juice and lashings of Africa's Solution.

During the first half of the film, fairly unsubtle product placement was used. Bottles of Africa's Solution with its distinctive yellow, green and black label were liberally displayed. In the second half, the marketing was much more overt, with Africa's Solution prescribed for every ailment on view. It could be taken orally or as ointment on ulcers and wounds. The refrain for the theme song, sung by a black man who accompanied himself on a drum, was 'African Solution'. There were also shots of health minister, Manto Tshabalala-Msimang who had, apparently, come to visit the project. Several scenes had her smiling encouragingly as various of Tine and Nelly's patients explained the miraculous cures the pair had wrought on them.

Towards the end of the film the local chief, Nkosi Bhengu, appeared on the screen, thanking them for their work. The credits at the end included ringing endorsements from branches of the National Association of people Living With Aids (NAPWA) and the Traditional Healers' Association.

I watched with a growing sense of outrage. The dreadful suffering of these people was only too evident. How dare these people play 'nursey nursey' with them?

When the last strains of African Solution had dwindled away and the lights had been switched on again, there was vigorous clapping from the hundred-odd-strong audience, but then a strange thing happened. Person after person got up to speak and it became clear that this was a gathering of a cult-like group, paranoid and beset by feelings of persecution. TAC was mentioned repeatedly and bitterly as the enemy, the tool of Big Pharma, the pharmaceutical mafia, well funded, powerful and ruthless. I arranged to meet Tine and Nelly the next day and made my escape.

The two women specified the café at Lifestyle, the garden centre on Beyers Naudé Drive, as a meeting place. It was convenient for them, they said, as a B&B nearby gave them a special rate and they used it as their base. I spotted them in the crowded café from way off, two furiously smoking, sturdy Dutchwomen surrounded by tables full of willowy, peroxide blonde housewives having a coffee before stocking up on a few plants.

Tine appeared to have forgiven me for the *Sunday Times* article, or maybe she was just desperate for any media interest, however suspect. She was, it transpired, hell-bent on getting this film screened on SABC TV. This was make or break time for her. Being ignored by the media seemed to be a painful experience for her. But, with this film – this evidence of the effectiveness of their method – she was convinced that finally they would get the recognition they deserved. All she had to do was get it on air.

Tine explained that the Inanda project was an indirect result of a Special Assignment TV programme which had examined her programme. Kim Cools, a Belgian who had established an organic farming project in Inanda, had contacted Tine after seeing her on TV. "At the time, we had our first paid work in five years," said Tine. "We were doing education for Coca-Cola – promoting our wellness programme." However, when the pair refused to promote anti-retrovirals, said Tine, they were fired. "We couldn't compromise."

"After ten days!" cackled Nelly. "It is quite something to be sixty-nine and to be fired for the first time in your life!" She and Tine laughed heartily. They laughed a lot. Laughter, they pointed out, was an essential element of their wellness programme, which they also refered to as 'the Lazarus programme'. This was not the first time I'd heard Lazarus's rise from the dead invoked in relation to Aids. I'd heard it from conventional doctors when referring to ARVs. There is clearly something about Aids that evokes promises of miracles.

Although they were Dutch, Tine and Nelly were both born in Argentina. When Tine was a few months old, they returned to Holland. In 1966, her father came out to South Africa under contract to work in the beer industry. His family accompanied him. Tine said that she remembered the shock of having to adapt to an Afrikaans school with its archaic attitudes to race, gender and corporal punishment. After school, she studied fine-art graphics at Port Elizabeth Technikon and then returned to Holland for several years. She came back to South Africa at the age of twenty-nine where she became a nurse. She got nursing jobs through agencies for a while and then Aids hit South Africa and a light went on for Tine. A friend in Holland became infected with HIV through her husband, who used to travel frequently to the Philippines. When it surfaced in South Africa, her mother, then back in Holland, sent information on Aids to Tine and, together, they began to work out an educational programme that would work in South African culture. "When I found Aids, my CV was about ten pages long because I had not found my passion," she said. Nelly came out from Holland and, together they formed First Aids Education Service, which set out to sell Aids awareness programmes to the corporate sector and the state.

Their 'wellness programme' essentially consisted of various combinations of lemons, olive oil, garlic, ginger and Africa's Solution (with regular doses of laughter). In her newsletter, Tine explained her commitment to Africa's Solution:"One of the most important things I have found that works like magic is Africa's Solution from Bermins and some of his other products. Over the years working with people living with HIV/Aids and other immune problems we have tried a lot of different supplements. Before we found Bermins, we taught people how to make a tea from the African potato, which is a tremendous immune booster. Picture the workings of the African potato this way: Normally, your white blood cells have a gun, and when an infection enters the body they shoot it … poof, poof. With the African potato your white blood cells have an AK-47. Now when an infection enters the body they shoot …rattattattattattatat. It makes the white blood cells much stronger. An extract from the African potato is in Bermins."

Tine and Nelly were proud of the fact that they had little formal education or training. Their remedies were homespun, evolved over the years and adjusted where required. A regular refrain from them was: "You must just use your imagination!"

Nellie, who said she trained, but has never worked, as a social worker, first learnt the value of non-traditional remedies from her Jewish grandparents. "When Tine was twelve, she got herpes in her eye. For a year, she was in and out of hospitals." Then Nellie's father suggested a remedy apparently used for generations by Jewish people: turtle doves. She bought a pair of turtle doves, put them in a cage and encouraged Tine to spend time with them. The herpes disappeared. "So we understood that turtle doves take it over but we don't know how," said Nellie.

Tine said: "We thought it's either the soapbox or a documentary. My mother didn't feel like the soapbox. So I phoned Kim and said how about if we do a documentary?" Kim had a camera and was willing. All they needed now were the ingredients for their programme. So Tine went on the internet, where she found ten suppliers of olive oil in the Cape. The first she tried agreed to donate 250 litres of olive oil. Bermins donated all the Africa's Solution they needed. Bokomo came up with Pronutro. The local Spar agreed to sell them lemons and garlic at cost. "Still, it was R1 for a lemon!" said Nelly.

Both continually emphasised their poverty. They said that they got no money from either the government or Bermins. "I have one pair of sandals and one pair of shoes," said Tine. "And there is only R4 000 left to draw on our credit card."

They hired a trailer, picked up the supplies from the various donors and set off for Inanda at the beginning of October, 2004. Kim explained that they needed to get clearance from the chief for their programme and, within a few days, they were given an audience. The chief, Nkosi Bhengu, said they could go ahead. They then started to look for patients. "In the beginning we had no patients. When we left, we had one hundred and sixty patients. People go where it works," said Tine.

"Our first patient was a *sangoma*. The history was: she got the big ill. She didn't know what her sickness was. We put her on the programme and after three days, she could walk." For the next twenty minutes, the pair bubbled away with examples of the awful illnesses they cured with their 'programme'. Their descriptions were earthy and full of amusement. They explained merrily that they gave their patients nicknames "because we can't remember Zulu names."

"For example, One Ball," said Tine. "He was also a *sangoma*. He had sugar [diabetes]. His one testicle had been amputated [hence the nickname] and his fingers were going. He had already paid five goats to another *sangoma* and he couldn't walk anymore." He was also impotent. "After two weeks [on the programme], he was back at work." What's more, his manhood was restored. "It's very important to a man, you know," said Tine gravely.

"We said: 'How's it going?'

"He said: 'It's only three times a week.' This is from nothing!

"We treated fifty-one with STDs that were not reacting to antibiotics. They all got better. For gonorrhea, you fill them up with garlic and Africa's Solution. With herpes, you mix lemon juice, aqueous cream and Disprin. We had a man with herpes on his penis. We gave him our cream: lemon juice is the active ingredient – and some Africa's Solution for the African potato; Disprin opens the pores; aqueous cream makes sure it goes in. You insert a clove of garlic in the vagina and in the anus."

Some of their descriptions sounded like something out of a freak show. "We had one man with a testicle the size of a small football! He had to lie with his legs open. You felt really sorry for that man. Another woman was shot in the stomach and something weird happened. She grew four more breasts! She was sent home [from hospital] with six breasts!"

Everyone was put on 'the programme', whatever the ailment. Nellie and Tine claimed to have cured cataracts, diabetes, high blood pressure and epilepsy in the four months they were there. All these miracles were filmed. With the permission of the patients, they emphasised. "They all signed they could go on TV. We said: 'What would you like to say to the people of South Africa?'"

'Dr Manto' as they called the health minister, came out twice to visit the project, said Tine. "That's why she keeps on saying lemons and garlic because she's seen it work."

Tine was convinced that, if they could only persuade the bigots in the media to show the film, the efficacy of their programme would be recognised. "That is why we made the documentary because all we wanted is that newspapers would publish the information so that people can read it and do the things and get well. But if you can't get that information out, you get as frustrated as an unmarried spinster!" said Tine with a hearty chuckle.

Their dream was to have their programme offered in all clinics and all hospitals. "If our programme is implemented in all the clinics, then the clinics will be empty. The hospitals will be empty because if you fix the malnourishment, you will fix all the problems."

Nellie said: "People believe HIV leads to Aids, Aids leads to death. You get the propaganda from TAC saying that unless you take anti-retrovirals you will die. At the hospital they get offered free of charge anti-retrovirals. Patients don't have a choice. With R120 – no liver tests – I can get them back to health. There is enormous resistance to ARVs. It is almost like a mafia. The ones who came on our programme were too scared to tell the doctors. So they fetch their anti-retrovirals. They hide them or they flush them through the toilet because somebody comes to inspect at the house: 'Did you take them?' It's like big brother watching."

Tine said she was a full dissident. She believed the symptoms attributed to Aids are in fact due to malnutrition – and should be treated accordingly. She said they do not actively encourage people not to take anti-retrovirals, but there was no doubt that she viewed anti-retroviral treatment as a rival to her programme and rubbished it at every opportunity. It was hard to imagine that she did not share these views with the people she treated.

"We actively say to people: go on our programme for three months. Then take anti-retrovirals if you want to. But when they've been on our programme for three months, they don't want anti-retrovirals. Why should they? They've put on weight. They're feeling well. Their skin is clear. Now people don't have a choice. They don't get told about our programme. They don't get told about the side effects [of ARVs]."

Their objections to anti-retrovirals were similar to those of most dissidents. HIV tests are suspect, anti-retrovirals breed resistance and give rise to unacceptable side effects. Their programme, on the other hand, was based on natural products, had no side effects and yet, they claimed, it was 90% effective in restoring patients to full health.

"What about Khabzela?" I asked Tine.

"Khabzela", she said decisively, "was killed by a combination of anti-retrovirals, whisky and pretnizone, an immune suppressant mistakenly prescribed to him by a doctor.

"Remember he was on them [anti-retrovirals] in May. And remember he was a huge whisky drinker [This is the first I'd heard of it. Fana favoured Hansa beer.] When I got him, his liver function was just above 20%. Professor Barnard says if it is below 20%, you've got no chance in hell of getting them through. Then, remember, he also had pretnizone, which is an immune depressant and is poison as hell. That was really bad. Then, when I left, they put him on anti-retrovirals."

She said she later went back to see Khabzela. "He couldn't even move his eyes any more. And I said straight to the family: 'He is going to die.' On our programme, there's no reason why you shouldn't die of old age."

Nellie broke in with an anecdote about how they got into a fight with some local thugs at Inanda. When one of them came at her with a broken bottle, she promptly picked up a Coke bottle full of olive oil and hit him over the head with it. The bottle broke and olive oil poured from it, soaking the thug and the area around him. Tine and Nelly roared with laughter when they recalled how he slipped in the oil and knocked himself out.

I left them after a couple of hours, both still furiously chain smoking, as they had throughout the meeting. I thought that in any other circumstances, I would consider them good value. They were full of hearty good humour, doughty and unconventional. I could picture them in an earlier era as lady missionaries, marching through Africa in panama hats and sturdy boots, saving the natives for Christ.

But I thought they had no place in a modern, democratic South Africa. I thought it a source of shame for us that they were given such ready access to desperately ill people to practise their potions on. Like many white people before them, they were using Africa's poverty to create a playground for themselves where they could play out their self-aggrandising fantasies. In Holland, they would not have been allowed to experiment on humans. Surely South Africans deserved the same respect?

# №̱ 20

By late April, 2005, Joburg was already gripped by the first chills of autumn. I had succumbed to one of the more vicious cold viruses in circulation so it seemed like a good time to head for the balmier climes of KwaZulu-Natal to check out Kim Cools in Inanda.

I found a mini-paradise. If Kim Cools' little commune had been situated anywhere but in the poverty-stricken, Aids-infested valleys of KZN, I'd have joined it like a shot. After months of harrowing immersion in Fana's life and death, my own soul felt badly in need of a little balm and here it was offered on a plate.

"I am a happy man," Kim confided as he took me on a tour of his property. And, indeed, he was a picture of well-being. With his slim, toned body and unlined face, he looked much younger than his forty-three years. There was no sign of grey in the light brown hair pulled back in a neat ponytail and his large, clear blue eyes radiated health. Kim Cools was a handsome, confident man, aglow with purpose.

Living with him on the commune were two much younger women who belonged to a non-governmental organisation called the Earthwomen. One was his wife, a South African of Indian origin. The other was Afrikaans. Both were attractive women, warm and engaging. They cooked a wonderful lunch over an open fire: pasta with soya mince and a hint of curry, garnished with fresh herbs and salad they had grown themselves. After lunch, they made me tea with freshly grated ginger to treat my cold. It was spicy and delicious and

I could feel the virus receding with every sip.

Kim's commune was situated on a little pensinsula that jutted out into the Inanda dam. He had erected a high fence topped with barbed wire across the border with the mainland, so it was, to all intents and purposes, a little island, cut off from the surrounding hills and the huts dotted all over them. Sometimes kids tried to access his property in boats to steal, he said. And for those eventualities, he kept an airgun to fire into the air to scare them off.

Kim and the earthwomen lived in brick and cement rondavels, surrounded by raised beds of vegetables. There were paw paw trees heavy with fruit and around the beds were dotted traditional gourds and urns, charmingly painted by the earthwomen. One of the rondavels was full of their paintings, mostly depicting the glories of nature. The whole place oozed fertility and creativity. At the tip of the peninsula were several smaller beds, which belonged to some local children, they explained. The children were let in for a couple of hours every evening to water and tend the beds.

They explained that they did not eat meat or drink alcohol. All their vegetables were organically grown – that is, without chemical fertilisers or pesticides. There was no electricity or running water on the property. The fridge was powered by gas. Cooking was done over open fires. There was a donkey shower on the edge of the lake and, a bit further away, a huge old bath propped up on bricks, with signs of a fire underneath and candle stubs around the edges. Water for the bath and shower were hauled from the lake, a couple of metres away. I could think of no better way of ridding myself of my ills than soaking in that bath for a few hours with its endless vistas over rippling water and softly rounded green hills.

In London, I worked for several years for the *Guardian*, a newspaper with a strong environmental and anti-globalisation lobby. Kim's vision would have found resonance with many of our readers (as it did with me, although I'd have drawn the line at having no meat or alcohol). Organic foods were hugely popular. They wanted to eat apples and carrots which hadn't been steeped in pesticides. They wanted meat that wasn't pickled in antibiotics and growth hormones. There was a deep antipathy towards genetically modified foods and alternative therapies such as homeopathy were much in demand despite a free and sophisticated conventional health service. Much of this was about a yearning for the purity and simplicity of the natural world, all but obliterated by the march of concrete in the industrialised north.

Kim's commune would have seemed like heaven on earth to many of them. But there was a serpent in this particular Garden of Eden that would rapidly poison its pleasures for me and, I suspect, for most *Guardian* readers. Kim was a rabid and active Aids dissident. He announced it on his business card which, alongside his name, contact details and occupation (which was given as Natural Health Consultant) was a strident slab of text labelled: SCIENTIFIC FACTS 'People are not dying from HIV; HIV is not the cause of Aids; Aids can be reversed 100%; ARVs are the cause of Aids death; GE/GMOs can cause Aids'.

He operated under the auspices of an NGO called the African Rainbow Circle and on his website was a page devoted to volunteers. He described himself as "a volunteer committed to bring facts to the people. Propaganda like that of the TAC and the pharma industry are the real reason for so-called Aids victims to eventually die. HIV does not cause

Aids and people with Aids can easily recover if they stop all sugar intake and eat right."

Above was the testimony of another 'volunteer' called Zonke. "I am HIV positive according to the so-called HIV test. I have been on ARVs for some time but since November 2004, I live better without ARVs and I advise all people to avoid these toxic drugs as they kill you slowly."

And then there were his views on black people. "White people are the disciplined people," he explained to me. "They are thinking with the left side of the brain which is the strategical side. The right side is what we used to work on – the emotional. When you act on gut feeling or emotion, which is always reliable. It is always right. If you are African you are driven by the right side of the brain. To be disciplined is to be not free and there is nothing worse for an African spirit than not being free. That is why the African will never succeed in this economy."

I wondered if he'd heard of Cyril Ramaphosa or Patrice Motsepe or even if he'd spoken to the black shopkeeper up the road. I wondered if he had shared his views with Manto Tshabalala-Msimang, whose smiling face beamed down on us from the noticeboard in Kim's office.

I asked Kim how he came by such a prime piece of real estate and he said matter of factly: "I told the king I would eradicate Aids and bring health and wealth to the area." In return, the 'king' told him he could pick any bit of land he wanted and gave him a ten-year lease, which could be extended to ninety-nine years. Kim said that no money exchanged hands.

The 'king' in question was Nkosi Bhengu, the local chief. And it was at his courthouse a couple of hills away that Kim and the earthwomen held their 'wellness' clinic. On Mondays and Thursdays, they promoted their views on HIV/Aids to local residents and sold them Tine and Nelly's cure-all diet of lemons, olive oil and garlic. They also provided a free meal – vegetarian, of course.

But, it seemed that the relationship between Tine and Kim was not as close as it had once been. They had fallen out over money. Kim said that one evening, after Tine had had a couple of whiskys, he inveigled out of her the information that she received R1 for every bottle of Africa's Solution that she sold. She promised to give his NGO one third of the money she received. This, Kim worked out, would be R1.5 million, based on the fact that there were five million people in South Africa with HIV, which would mean R5 million to Tine and a third of her share to him. He said he had already told the king about this expected bounty and then, when Tine and Nelly got back from a two-week Christmas break at their Bloemfontein home, Tine denied all knowledge of the conversation. The promise of R1.5 million had disappeared.

Since then, Kim had been looking to make his own immune booster to replace Africa's Solution. I found this conversation fascinating as it threw a whole new light on Tine's motivation. She had always insisted that she did not benefit financially from her promotion of Africa's Solution.

The district hospital which served the Inanda district was St Mary's, a large, airy former mission hospital situated in the lush green hills of Marianhill, twenty kilometres from Durban. In their literature, St Mary's pointed out that KwaZulu-Natal was the epicentre of the HIV epidemic. Their catchment area included about 750 000 people. It was a very poor rural area and unemployment was around 60%. One in three adults was thought to be HIV positive. The infection rate among pregnant women attending the hospital's ante-natal clinic was 59%. Three quarters of their patients tested HIV positive.

St Mary's conducted an intensive Aids awareness programme which includeed the following information, tailored to counter the myths prevalent in their area: 'Aids is not caused by a curse or bewitchment. It is not caused by poor nutrition. HIV is not spread by mosquitoes. You can't be infected by casual contact from living with a person with HIV. You cannot be cured by sleeping with a virgin. Currently there is no effective vaccine for HIV. There is currently no cure for HIV but anti-retrovirals, a combination of three medicines, help strengthen the immune system and allow an HIV-positive person to live a healthy life.'

In 2003, St Mary's began offering ARVs at its iThemba Family Care Centre. It also obtained funding to enrol one hundred new patients a month on its ARV programme. To qualify, patients needed to have a CD4 count of below 200 and they had to have told at least one other person close to them that they had Aids in order to get the necessary support to stay on the programme. It was explained that once ARVs were started, they had to be continued for life. If they were started and stopped, resistance to the drugs would develop and they would no longer work.

Nancy Sias ran the Community Outreach programme at iThemba. I asked her what impact, if any, Kim's proselytising had on the work of the clinic.

"They have really presented a challenge to us," she said. "Most people there are illiterate and very gullible, especially if it's a white man."

Working under Nancy were several adherence counsellors, who visited the homes of patients on ARVs every month to ensure they were taking them properly. I met two of them. They were sweet, gentle young women who clearly did not find their job easy. But these must have been the sinister agents of 'Big Brother' Tine and Nelly had referred to so scathingly.

I headed back to the chief's court where Kim and the earthwomen were conducting their Thursday clinic. Kim was sitting in his office, with five or six young black people sitting opposite him. On his desk were bottles of olive oil and lemon juice, left over from that morning's clinic. Beside them was a cardboard box which Kim called his HIV box. In it were empty chip packets, Coca-Cola tins and boxes of soup mix. These were all the things that indirectly caused Aids, according to Kim.

He introduced me to the young people sitting opposite him, one of whom was a young woman who Kim proudly told me had stopped taking ARVs three months before.

"No, six months," she corrected him.

"Six months," said Kim triumphantly. "And look how well she looks!"

Kim had told me earlier that he was not in this for the long haul. "Within two years, I'll be gone," he said.

I thought, as with Tine and Nelly, that there was an overweening arrogance at play here. He had claimed – indeed promised – "to eradicate Aids and bring health and wealth" to this destitute area. And all within another two years! But I also thought of Nancy and her adherence counsellors trekking around these hills trying to counter his propaganda and I thought that to them, two years might seem like an awfully long time.

# № 21

It was through a small, photocopied invoice in Fana's file at Yfm that I discovered he had had a consultation with David Spencer. I was excited when I saw this because Dr Spencer was one of the most highly regarded HIV clinicians in the country. At some point at least, Fana had had access to first class conventional treatment. Yet this discovery also deepened the mystery around his death. If he had been treated by someone of this calibre, why did he die? The answer, as it turned out, was that he saw the doctor but did not listen to him.

David Spencer was a physician with a background in cancer and blood disorders. He trained in the field of Infectious Diseases in the USA in the late 1980s. At the end of 1991, he took over the Infectious Diseases Clinic at Johannesburg Hospital. Previously this clinic had catered for a small number of mainly gay white men who were HIV positive and required support and medical assistance. Many returning exiles and refugees were found to be HIV infected and required help. At the same time the numbers of local people infected with the virus also started increasing. This was the mid-1990s. Since then, Dr Spencer had been immersed in HIV, becoming one of the country's foremost experts. He trained doctors and nurses throughout southern Africa and headed a private medical practice that specialised in the care of HIV-infected people. It was there that he saw Fana.

As a middle-aged white man, David Spencer did not exactly fall into Yfm's target audience and had never heard of Khabzela when the latter walked into his consulting rooms in September 2003. The consultation was extremely brief. Nevertheless his encounter with Fana was still etched in his mind. "I remember that particular incident because it was so bizarre," he said. "He was difficult. He came in with an attitude. He said: 'I'm HIV positive and I want treatment but you can't use anti-retrovirals on me!' I replied that I didn't treat HIV with diet or herbs. He stalked out. It was a totally unsatisfactory encounter. He was in my office for less than a minute.

"It took me about another minute to get over his reaction. When I came to my senses I went outside to see if he had brought someone with him with whom I could reason. He had gone and we had no telephone or contact numbers. He was hostile, an angry young man. I thought he must be demented. Aids encephalitis, for example, is a condition that often causes people to behave in aggressive or unpredictable ways."

Dr Spencer said the incident had stayed with him and he wondered later whether his failure to recognise Fana might have contributed to his attitude. "I just took him as another human being. I did not treat him as a celebrity."

I told him about the alternative therapies Fana had tried before and after he saw him. Dr Spencer did not hide his disgust. "I'm sick and tired of these people," he said. "They are like parasites feeding on the carcass of HIV and Aids."

The fact that Fana had repeatedly had his hopes raised and dashed by ostensible miracle cures might well have contributed to his anger, he said. Dr Spencer said that there were a whole range of products all purporting to boost the immune system but because they were classified as food supplements they did not require approval by bodies such as the Medicines Control Council (MCC) or, in America, the Food and Drug Administration (FDA). "They should go through rigorous testing," he said. "We need the truth that comes from evidence-based scientific research to back up claims about their effectiveness. Then we, the care-givers and our patients, are on level ground. Without this there is no accountability.

"In fact there is growing evidence that so called 'natural remedies' and even foods taken in excessive quantities can do harm. The consumption of raw garlic cloves has been shown to diminish the absorption of drugs, including anti-retrovirals," he said. "It is naïve to assume that foodstuffs are without any biological activity. The so-called immune boosters such as the African potato and Sutherlandia impair the metabolic activity of the anti-retrovirals and the use of the African potato in Aids patients has been documented to worsen their CD4 cell counts. I advise extreme caution when talking to patients who wish to take these things.

"The medicine used by traditional healers has not, to the best of my knowledge, been subjected to any reasonable scrutiny. It is difficult to know where such care-givers and their medication fit into the support of the HIV-infected person. A common thread as I see it, is that of counselling and the provision of psychological support to patients. Both Western-trained doctors and traditional healers have some degree of expertise in these areas. Western medicine is based upon the germ theory and has a very credible record in the western world. It seems to me that there is a retreat in the face of this knowledge. We act as if we have nothing really to offer the HIV infected. But since the mid-1990s we've had drugs that control this virus and keep people well."

I said that, in November, Fana had had a CD4 count of 2. "Would any therapy have made a difference at that point?" He said:"I have patients who came with extremely low CD4 counts in the late 1990s and are now well on the anti-retrovirals. When the medication is taken reliably there is generally no reason why patients can't live a further ten to twenty years. I do lose patients at times. Some come too late and have irreversible damage already. Others seem to lack the will to face life and appear to give up. The anti-retrovirals do have side-effects and may cause harm in some. That's why I insist that the patient must followup in a clearly defined manner. Particularly in the early stages of commencing anti-retroviral therapy patients need a lot of support and understanding. But in most cases they rapidly regain their appetites and start to gain weight and feel better within the first several weeks."

# № 22

I had by now collected reams of paper recording Fana's treatment at various hospitals. I decided to reproduce an edited version of them them here because it seemed to me that there was still so much mystification around Aids and what it actually does to the human body. Fana was always so open about his life, so willing to use his own experience to help others. I hoped, therefore, that he would not have objected to my publishing this record of what HIV did to him.

Fana was admitted to the Brenthurst Clinic Intensive Care Unit on 14/09/03. His next of kin was given as his fiancée, Sibongile Radebe. There was a copy of the front page of Fana's ID book and a promise to pay the hospital's bill. Dirk Hartford of Yfm, The Zone, Rosebank acted as guarantor.

Initial assessments read: 'Patient immuno-compromised. Very weak. Complaining of a pain in the left arm and shoulder. Urinary catheter inserted. Rash over the whole body. Looks clean but smelling. Very depressed. Responsive and awake. Communicating well. Skin status: intact.'

A doctor examined him and diagnosed HIV-dementia and cryptococcal (fungal) meningitis. He ordered a chest x-ray and a spinal tap to confirm the diagnosis of meningitis. The test was negative. Fana did not have a fungal meningitis.

## Nursing records

15/09/03

07.00 hrs: 'Patient handed over in a stable condition. He has non-productive cough and has passed a considerable amount of urine. He is eating well and drinking well but experiencing continuous diarrhoea. Immodium (an anti-diarrhoeal agent) and supplementary fluids were given.'

13.00 hrs: 'Doctor came to see the patient and review the results of the CSF (spinal fluid analysis), blood tests and the chest x-ray. He was told about the high temperature. He stopped the anti fungal medication and started him on a broad spectrum intravenous antibiotic. To do: shoulder x-ray and collect sputum as patient is still coughing.'

He was put on the anti-retrovirals Combivir and Viramune, and on anti-tuberculosis (TB) drugs. Later, Africa's Solution forte; Imuwize forte and Imutain were added to the patient's intravenous therapies.

18.00 hrs: 'The patient is haemodynamically stable but has a rapid pulse rate and a fever at 39.5°C. He is passing good amounts of urine through his catheter but is still having loose stools. He is eating reluctantly.'


16/09/03

7.20 hrs: 'The patient is not well, asleep but stable. Breathing well on room air. But still has a fever.'

19.10 hrs: 'Patient appears to be 'dull' and ill-looking. He is moving both his upper and lower limbs. However his stomach appears distended. Refusing a naso-gastric tube and removing his oxygen mask.'

24.00 hrs: 'Patient not sleeping most of the night.'

17/09/03

22.00 hrs: 'The patient is calling out and requesting that a lot of things be done to him. He asked for a cup of tea and two slices of bread. These were given but he took very little. He is coughing productively. He is also scratching, especially the face and head.'

0600: 'Insomnia. Calling out throughout the night.'


18/09/03

19.00 hrs: 'Aggressive and confused all day. Found naked and to have removed and thrown away all connections.'

20.00 hrs: 'Patient reconnected without any resistance; dressed with gown and covered nicely.'

22.00 hrs: 'Position changed and attention given to pressure points: the patient has a 'threatening' sore on left heel.'

06.00 hrs: 'Slept throughout the night but has a tendency to pull out leads and the blood pressure cuff. Still coping without oxygen.'


A nurse's report on 18/09/03 recorded regular turns to prevent bed sores; intensive psychological care and 'the patient needs teaching and conditioning'.


On 20/09/03, the doctor prescribed the anti-TB drug, Rifafour; the antibiotic Tequin, and a vitamin, vitamin B6, Pyridoxine.


On 21/09/03, he was discharged with a bill of R12 463.36 and a diagnosis of 'neuropathy, tuberculosis'. His condition was described as 'stable'.

At this point, Fana had advanced HIV infection with widespread disease of the brain and possibly of the spinal cord. His irrational behaviour could well have been caused by the virus attacking his brain. Damage to areas that control a person's thought processes and their emotions can result in very irrational behaviour, mood and personality changes. Where the damage is to those areas of the brain that control movement and where the spinal cord is involved, the patient may become paralysed or have a stroke. Even the control of the bladder and the bowels may be lost.

As soon as he was back home, Fana went off the ARVs. The following month, Manto Tshabalala-Msimang sent Tine to look after him. After her departure, he deteriorated so alarmingly that the family admitted him to a private hospital in Soweto. He was suffering from an HIV-related inflammation of the bowel (colitis) which caused chronic diarrhoea and haemorrhaging. Part of his intestine was removed to stop the bleeding and the remaining intestine diverted to deliver his faecal waste to a bag (colostomy bag) placed on the front of his abdomen.

Fearful of the mounting costs, the family removed him from the private hospital in Soweto and he was admitted to Johannesburg Hospital on 30/12/03.

A doctor from the Soweto hospital wrote a letter of referral:

RE: Fana Khaba: patient with RVD (retroviral disease) and complications.

Presenting:

'Bedridden, moribund, unable to walk/move limbs – neuropathy. Transfused 26/12/03 four units; 30/12/03 3 units.

Colostomy in situ – working well

Catheter draining well

Intermittent memory lapses.'

Large sacral bedsore; multiple other bedsores: hips, elbows. back, ankles etc."

On 31/12/03, doctors at Johannesburg Hospital wrote:

'History difficult. Progressive onset of weakness in legs then arms over months. Cognitively: poor attention/ concentration.'

And then, the rather heartbreaking line: 'Main problem now is pain.'

On 02/01/04

'Advanced RVD; HIV dementia; neuropathy.'

On 03/01/04

'Advanced RVD; HIV dementia; myelopathy; neuropathy; TB; bedridden – bed sores.

No new complaints.'

On 05/01/04

He is pronounced 'clinically stable'.

On 06/01/04, a doctor's notes read: 'A thirty-four-year-old male who has advanced retroviral disease with HIV neuropathy; myelopathy, dementia and bedsores. He is currently on anti-retroviral therapy (ART) and TB medicines. He has a colostomy and a laparotomy wound which had been closed with staples and extensive bedsores. He is currently awaiting a CT brain scan on 16/01/04.'

On 07/01/04: 'The patient wants to go home.'

On 08/01/04
'Pain well controlled on current meds.
Patient awake; not oriented; hallucinating'

On 09/01/04
'Patient can't keep eyes open.'

On 11/01/04
'Colostomy – bloody
Bed sores – extensive
Awaiting CT brain scan 16/01/04.'

12/01/04
'Got verbal consent for CT brain scan Friday. Patient too weak to sign.'

13/01/04
'Patient very disoriented today. Plebotomist unable to take bloods.'

14/01/04
05h30:
'about 500ml of blood has leaked from colostomy bag.
Patient disorientated. Not responding to verbal commands.

Bed sore buttocks – extensive – complete loss of gluteus maximus muscle – infected.'

11h00:

'Patient bleeding from colostomy and urine is blood stained.

Patient unresponsive. Call surgeon.'

12h10:

"Pulse palpable

Pupils fixed and dilated

Unresponsive to light

Patient pronounced dead.

Time of death: 12h15.'

On the death certificate, Fana's cause of death was given as: 'Advanced retroviral disease'. In other words, Aids.

Fana's final days must have been a nightmare. He would have been in severe pain, bedridden and covered in suppurating sores. He had lost his ability to defecate and urinate. He had all but lost his mind.

# Conclusion

It is early June 2005, and I sit at my desk gazing out through open French doors at a dragonfly fluttering metallic-blue wings over the paler blue of the swimming pool. Yellow weaver birds swoop in and out of overhanging branches. A lizard lies immobile beside the pool, baking in the sun. The only sound I can hear is the cheerful cooing of a resident dove.

I've been back in South Africa for more than two years now and I still wake up every day grateful that I am living in this country and that it is being run by the ANC. Unlike before I left, when things just kept getting worse, now they just keep on getting better. The body politic overall seems to be wise, progessive, intelligent. I had a brief glimpse of such a government in the first few years under Tony Blair until he spoiled it all by becoming a warmonger. Now, give me Thabo Mbeki rather than Tony Blair any day.

With one exception. My journey through Fana Khaba's life has made government policy as regards the HIV/Aids epidemic personal.

I understand and appreciate Thabo Mbeki's belief that HIV is profoundly different here to what it is in the West. His insistence that poverty and malnutrition are a crucial element is undoubtedly correct. Anti-retrovirals are useless to someone dying of starvation. He is right to reject the cynical and greedy agendas of the pharmaceutical companies. I wholeheartedly support his preference for an African response to a very African manifestation of the epidemic.

But what puzzles me is the collection of dodgy Europeans who appear to have been given succour by his minister of health. Tine and Nelly van der Maas and Kim Cools are Dutch and Belgian respectively. What's more, a Belgian who propagates the view that black people are genetically incapable of functioning in a modern economy. How does this square with the African renaissance? Does all one have to do to gain credence is attach the word African to something: African potato? Africa's Solution? African Rainbow Circle?

This polarisation of the debate between ARVs on the one hand and nutrition on the other is not only a false debate – because clearly both ARVs and good nutrition are required – but it also means that little else is discussed.

In the last couple of years before I left Britain, Thabo Mbeki was a hate figure because of his views on HIV. All his other achievements, everything else he did to make this country the stable, dynamic, successful place it is, got lost behind that one issue. He was viewed as a nutcase at best, a genocidal monster at worst. A lot of this was racist, I thought: the West is all too ready to come up with stereotypes of Africans as irrational, primitive, hopeless.

Never, in all the acres of newsprint and film footage devoted to his views on Aids was there a word about South Africans' own deeply ambivalent views on the subject. Nor do I see much about it in the media here. Public discourse about HIV/Aids is limited to the provision or not of anti-retrovirals. The vast grey area in between is virtually ignored.

My journey through Fana Khaba's life has made me realise how complex are South Africans' own responses to HIV/Aids. Fana was a modern, urban, cosmopolitan man. He was exposed to as much education about HIV as he needed

– indeed, he dispensed it himself. All his life, he refused to follow the herd. An independent mind like this is unlikely to have been susceptible to the views of a politician, such as the health minister, particularly on a matter which affected his own survival.

Access to anti-retrovirals was not an issue. Compassionate employers saw to it that he would be able to afford them. Yet Fana rejected them and despite all the questions I've asked and the often very perceptive answers I've received, essentially all this book has done for me is deepen the mystery around his death.

And I know he is not alone. There are many others who make the same choices every day.

When Fana first became ill, he believed he had been bewitched. This, I discovered, is not an unusual response. He had a profound distrust of western medicines – which is, again, not uncommon. In Europe, ever-increasing numbers of people seek so-called natural therapies such as homeopathy and Chinese medicine in preference to modern drugs. In this country, where physical and emotional problems are often considered to be linked, traditional healing methods are very popular. It has been estimated that 80% of South Africans' first port of call is a traditional healer. It doesn't seem to me to be an outrageously high estimate.

People with by HIV are confronted, as Fana was, by a range of options, many of them unhealthy ones. There are so many people in this field claiming to be acting purely out of altruism. Many are, I'm sure. But many more also see Aids as a business opportunity. Following the money trail, doing an audit of exactly who is making how much money out of Aids would help to create transparency and expose vested interests.

The more information we all have, the better.

HIV/Aids is not a simple ailment, nor one which the pharmaceutical companies can claim to have conquered. All they have come up with are drugs to stave off the virus, not to eradicate it. These involve a complex regimen which many doctors have yet to get to grips with. The syndrome itself is a many-headed beast which initially manifests in a bewildering variety of ways: headaches, paralysed limbs, shingles, TB, pneumonia, meningitis. Each could quite easily be unconnected to HIV. When do you start gathering the courage to take the test which might change your life forever? If you test positive, the prospect of death will have entered your life even if, as in Fana's case, it has only just begun.

I think that township spiritual eclecticism, so enriching in other ways might, in the case of HIV/Aids, be counter-productive. The urgency of impending death drove Fana's family to try an ever wider range of remedies: prayer, traditional healers, white miracle pedlars as well as ARVs, when in fact what they needed was an unequivocal orthodoxy.

Fana Khaba has been dead just over a year now. I'm hoping that this book, with all the invasion of his and others' lives it has entailed, will serve some purpose. That it will help to open up the debate. That it will show the many thousands of people who loved and admired him the consequences of his choices and help them to make better ones.

Let them look perhaps at my little boy, who, thanks to anti-retrovirals – and excellent nutrition – has just celebrated his fifth birthday and has all but caught up on the development lost during his early years of illness.

Let them look at Sibongile, determined to make a life for herself despite the virus waiting to ambush her. Her apprenticeship at the travel agent is going well. She has a new boyfriend who is loving and supportive. She eats well and exercises regularly. She is doing everything she can to make sure she stays as well as possible for as long as possible. And when the time comes that she does need anti-retrovirals, she will have no hesitation in taking them. Meanwhile, she is going to embrace life. "Fana always lived life to the full," she said. "And that is what I am going to do."

And she's right. He did. The fact that Fana's life ended in tragedy should not obscure the fact that he lived an extraordinary life in extraordinary times, and that he made a difference. Not many people can claim that.

*Lala kahle*, Fana Khaba. May you rest in peace.

# Bibliography

Achille Mbembe, Nsizwa Dlamini and Grace Khunou: *Soweto Now* (Public Culture, volume 16, number 3, Fall 2004)

Belinda Bozzoli with the assistance of Mmantho Nkotsoe: *Women of Phokeng: consciousness, life strategy and migrancy in South Africa 1900-1983* (Ravan 1991)

Clive Glaser: *Bo Tsotsi: The Youth Gangs of Soweto 1935-1976* (Heinemann 2000)

Christopher Ballantine: 'Popular music and the end of Apartheid: the Case of Kwaito' (paper presented at the conference of the International Association for Popular Music, Montreal 2003)

Edwin Cameron: *A Witness to Aids* (Tafelberg 2005)

Janet Malcolm: *In the Freud Archives* (Papermac 1997)

Janet Malcolm: *The Journalist and the Murderer* (Papermac 1998)

Meshack M Khosa: 'Taxi revolution on the rocks?' (Indicator SA, Vol 13, No 2 1996)

Mia Brandel-Syrier: *Reeftown Elite: A study in Social Mobility in a Modern African Community on the Reef* (Routledge & Keegan Paul 1971)

Nelson Mandela: *Long Walk to Freedom* (Macdonald Purnell 1994)

Philip Bonner and Lauren Segal: *Soweto, A History* (Maskew Miller Longman 1998)

Sarah Nuttall: 'Stylizing the Self: the Y Generation in Rosebank, Johannesburg' (Public Culture, volume 16, number 3, Fall 2004)

The Kwaito Nation: 'An Industry Analysis' (Yfm)

www.yfm.co.za

*Watchtower* (August 1, 2004)

'Top radio jock says he is HIV positive' (*Sunday Times* 18/5/2003)

'Ailing but defiant DJ Khabzela accepts award' (13/12/2003)

'Health minister saddened by Khaba death' (18/1/2204)

'Picture of Sibongile' (*Sunday World* 25/1/2004)

'Soweto bids Khaba a tearful goodbye' (*Sunday Times*, 25/1/2004)

'Condolences, tributes pour in for deejay Khabzela' (*The Star* 15/1/2004)

'Caring for Khaba' (*Sunday World* 26/10/2003)

'Khabzela mourners urged to vote' (*Sunday World* 25/1/2004)

'Khabzela – an inspiring hero of the airwaves' (1/2/2004)

---

Aids Helpline 0800 012 322
www.aidsinfo.co.za